Secrets of the

iPod

Second Edition

Christopher Breen

Peachpit Press • Berkeley, California

Secrets of the iPod, Second Edition

Christopher Breen

Peachpit Press

1249 Eighth Street
Berkeley, CA 94710
510/524-2178
800/283-9444
510/524-2221 (fax)
Find us on the World Wide Web at: http://www.peachpit.com
Peachpit Press is a division of Addison Wesley Longman

Editor: Nancy Peterson
Production Coordinator: Connie Jeung-Mills
Copyeditor: Kathy Simpson
Compositor: Owen Wolfson
Indexer: Karin Arrigoni
Cover Design: George Mattingly, GMD
Cover Illustration: Ben Fishman, Artfish Inc.

ISBN 0-321-16783-X

9 8 7 6 5 4 3 2 1

To my own little iBreen, Addie.

Acknowledgements

This book wouldn't be in your hands if not for the hard work and care of the following individuals.

At Peachpit Press: My editor and pal, Nancy Peterson (who, in addition to making sense of my nonsense, ran interference while I clacked out the last couple of chapters); Cliff Colby (who edited a fair chunk of the first edition, accepted the idea that we needed a second edition two weeks after the first shipped, and proffered the original idea for an iPod book); Marjorie Baer (who gave the green light for the first edition); Rebecca Ross (who handled the contract negotiations with such aplomb); Nancy Ruenzel (Peachpit's publisher, who signed off on another go-round of this book); Kathy Simpson (who copyedited both editions of the book and made some brilliant catches in each); Connie Jeung-Mills (who, under enormous pressure, pulled all the pieces together without once sending me an email that began "Excuse me, but do you have *any* idea how close we are to missing the press date!?"); Kim Lombardi (who is a book-promoting machine); and Kelly Ryer (who bought an iPod at the right time and asked all the right questions).

At home: My wife, Claire, who once again kept the other parts of our lives together while I clacked on heedlessly in the basement; and the boys of System 9 for being such groovy cats.

Abroad: The many vendors who supplied the swag...er, *test units* of the products mentioned in these pages: BookEndz, Dr. Bott, Griffin Technology, Now Software, Joe Masters (EphPod), Mediafour, SiK Inc., Waterfield Designs, and XtremeMac. Sam Braff for coming through in a pinch. The folks behind the coolest iPod Web sites around: iPoding (*www.ipoding.com*) and iPodlounge (*www.ipodlounge.com*). Alicia Awbrey at Apple and Katy Saeger at MusicMatch for answering my questions so quickly. Keri Walker at Apple, who not only saw to it that I received the iPod test units I needed, but also was very forgiving when, many months ago, I admitted to her that I'd intentionally destroyed one of her beta units. Finally, of course, the designers behind the iPod. Beautiful work!

Table of Contents

Introduction

It was with a mixture of elation and bitter disappointment that I listened to Apple's charismatic CEO, Steve Jobs, deliver his keynote speech on the morning of July 17, 2002, at Macworld Expo in New York City. Elation, because Mr. Jobs announced that Apple's immensely popular digital music player, the iPod, had been revised to include a new 20 GB model, bundled remote-control units and cases with the 10 and 20 GB models, and new calendar and clock functions. Apple would also be issuing a Microsoft Windows-compatible version of the iPod.

And my reason for disappointment? The first edition of this book had shipped just two weeks before Expo. In an instant, my brand-new book was out of date.

Never one to be derailed by such disappointment, I quickly realized that I had the wondrous opportunity to champion the iPod outside the Macintosh community. (But jeez, Steve, before the next revision, how about giving your old buddy Chris a call?) Windows users, perhaps leery of Apple products in the past, would have a chance to see that there's something to all this talk about Apple's design philosophy—that Apple really does know how to create an intuitive interface and design elegant (and functional) products.

At the same time, I could expand on some of the information in the first edition, as well as reveal all that's worth knowing about the iPod's new features.

Looks like Steve did me a favor after all.

And exactly what makes the iPod so worthy of our attention? There are its weight and size, of course—a scant 6.5 ounces for the 5 and 10 GB models (the 20 GB model weighs 7.2 ounces) and no larger than a pinochle deck. Also, the 20 GB model holds 4,000 four-minute songs for a playing time of 11 full days (or *more* if you follow the tips in this book).

But most impressive of all is the simplicity of the device. Like so many Apple products before it, the iPod is most astonishing for its elegant design and ease of use. There just isn't a more beautiful or intuitive music player available today.

Best of all, the iPod has other wonders to behold than just its capability to pump out a few thousand toe-tapping tunes.

In these pages, I'll reveal all the iPod's wonders—from managing your music collection to keeping your contacts and appointments close at hand. Macintosh users will learn about the intimate relationship between the i-siblings—iPod and iTunes—and how to make the most of that relationship. And Windows users will discover a similar symbiotic relationship between their iPod and MusicMatch Jukebox. I'll examine the iPod as a storage device for your computer and show you how to dress up your iPod with the latest accessories. And when you're finished with the outside, I'll take you on a tour of the iPod's innards, scrutinizing what makes this machine tick (and what can keep it from ticking) and offering troubleshooting tips for those times when the music inexplicably stops.

In short, this smallish tome will cover the iPod from its shiny little bottom to its port-bearing top.

iPod, Therefore iAm

Before eyeballing the ins and outs of the iPod, it's worth taking a step back and asking the question "Why iPod?"

With all the wondrous devices to which Apple might have devoted its legendary creative power, why create yet another music player? To learn the answer to this question, you must look at a technology that has changed the way we use and share digital media: MP3.

The MP3 revolution

In 1987, a German company, Fraunhofer IIS-A, began working on a system for creating digital audio files that consumed little storage space while maintaining much of the original file's quality. Among other things, this work was motivated by the fact that one minute of CD-quality stereo music consumed about 10 MB of storage space—storage space that at the time was very costly. The eventual result of this work was something called the MPEG Audio Layer-3 compression standard (now commonly known as MP3).

This standard uses *perceptual coding* techniques to eliminate audio data that the human ear is unlikely to discern. So efficient is MP3 encoding that you can use it to reduce an audio file's size by a factor of 12 and maintain most of the sound quality of the original file. Thanks to MP3, a four-minute song that normally would devour 40 MB of available hard drive space now weighs in at less than 4 MB.

The availability of more-compact and less-expensive storage media—hard drives and media cards—made MP3 an attractive option for use on home computers and, eventually, portable music players. But the fact that such files were easier to store was only one piece of the puzzle. MP3 really came into its own thanks to the widespread dispersal of a seemingly unrelated technology: broadband Internet access.

In the days when much of the world accessed the Internet with slothlike modems, downloading a 4 MB file could be an all-night affair. When that file could be downloaded in a minute, the idea of moving high-quality audio files across the Internet became an extremely attractive proposition—particularly among college students who had both lightning-fast, school-supplied access to the Internet and a keen interest in music.

Given that MP3 was a growing concern among such a significant portion of the population, manufacturers of audio devices predictably began seeking ways to incorporate MP3 technology into future products.

Share and share alike

Anyone with the faintest interest in technology has heard of the Napster music-sharing service, through which audio files—largely encoded with MP3—were swapped wholesale across the Internet (much to the chagrin of the recording industry). Music-device manufacturers understood that although those who downloaded MP3 files were pleased enough to play back these files on their computers, many would be even more pleased if they could transport and listen to these files on a portable device.

After the courts determined that such devices were indeed legal—that they were not specifically designed as go-between devices that might aid music piracy, but as a final destination for music files—small MP3 players such as the Rio 600 found their way to market. Regrettably, these players stored less than an hour of music without the addition of expensive media storage cards. (And even with these additional storage cards, such players rarely exceeded two hours' playing time.) Moving MP3 files from the computer to the player over the player's slow serial-port or USB connection could take a long time, and the software required to move files from one device to another was hardly intuitive. Navigating from song to song on these things was a tedious affair, requiring you to page through menu after menu on a tiny screen. Finally, these players cost upward of a couple of hundred dollars. Although the technology was interesting, only gearheads with more money than sense were likely to replace their inexpensive portable CD players with one of these devices.

Even with these limitations, portable MP3 players still sold in respectable numbers. But just imagine the kind of sales you could generate if you created a portable music player that successfully worked around the storage, transfer-rate, and navigation problems.

Apple smelled an opportunity.

iPod, arise!

On October 23, 2001, Apple held a press conference in Cupertino, California, to announce a new product—the first noncomputer product released by Apple since the ill-fated console gaming system, Pippin, and the first such product produced since Apple co-founder Steve Jobs returned to the company. Web-based rumor sites were rife with speculation about the new device. Would it be a revolutionary personal-information manager? An advanced console computing system? The ultimate toaster oven?

When Mr. Jobs ended the speculation and revealed the iPod at a press conference, some of those in attendance were disappointed initially. "Sure, it stores a ton of music, offers loads of battery life, transfers files in an instant, and is easy to use (and easy on the eyes). But after all the hype, you've called us here to show off an *MP3 player*? And you want *how much* for it!? You must be joking!"

Then Apple did a very smart thing. At the end of the event, each person in attendance was handed an iPod of his or her very own.

Cynics among us might suggest that Apple attempted to curry favor and lessen the shock of the iPod's $399 price tag by offering members of the press free swag. Far from it. The folks at Apple understood that to truly appreciate the iPod, you had to hold it in your hand, admire its sleek design, swiftly wheel through its menus, and absorb its rich sound.

The tactic worked. Although nearly every review of the iPod mentioned that $399 was a lot of money for a music player, few disputed the notion that similar devices were clunky and crude in comparison.

Despite the price and the fact that it worked best only with the assistance of a Macintosh computer, the iPod became *the* music player to own—so much so, in fact, that Apple sold 125,000 of them in the iPod's first 60 days of existence, and people who had never considered owning a Mac bought one simply so they could use it with the iPod.

In March 2002, Apple released a second iPod model that featured a 10 GB hard drive (versus the original's 5 GB drive). Although many people hoped that subsequent iPod models would be less expensive than the original, this second iPod iteration cost $499—$100 more. Lessening the sting was the accompanying iPod Software Update 1.1, which made the iPod more functional by including such features as the ability to keep contacts on your iPod, music *scrubbing* (a feature for accurately navigating forward and backward through a song as it plays), on-board equalization (the process of boosting or cutting certain audio frequencies, also known as *EQ)*, and the option to shuffle playback by song or album. Apple also announced that when customers ordered from the online Apple Store, both the 5 and 10 GB models could be engraved with two lines of text (27 characters per line, including spaces and punctuation) for an additional $49.

On October 17, 2002, a new generation of iPods was announced. This group included the $299 5 GB model, the $399 10 GB iPod, and the $499 20 GB unit. In addition to new prices and a higher-capacity model, the features that distinguished this passel of music players were the ability to keep calendar information on the iPod, a new touch-sensitive scroll wheel (previous models included a wheel that turned, whereas the wheel on the new units doesn't turn), redesigned earbuds that fit smaller ear canals more comfortably, support for Audible.com content (Mac version only), a FireWire port cover, and inclusion of a wired remote control and carrying case on the 10 and 20 GB models. Apple also welcomed PC users into the iPod fold by issuing models that were compatible with Windows.

The iPod's future

What's next? More -comprehensive data management? A color display for viewing pictures and movies? A software update that turns the erstwhile music player into a handheld gaming device? Only Apple can say for sure where the iPod's future lies. But given Apple's inclination for innovation, it's a safe bet that today's iPod is only the beginning.

And what a beginning it's been.

Contents, Controls, and Interface

You've just placed your online order for an iPod with the Apple Store and are counting the seconds before the big brown truck pulls up to your door and delivers your little digital wonder. To prepare you for what you'll find when you tear the shrink wrap from the package (and, perhaps, to slow you down enough to keep you from suffering paper cuts), I'll examine what you'll discover inside the box; what those things do; and how to charge your iPod, use its controls, and—using those controls—find your way around the interface.

Contents

If you can contain your excitement, take time to linger over unwrapping the iPod's box. The packaging is as beautifully designed as the iPod itself—from the elegant and understated outer sleeve to the inner box that folds open like a jewelry case.

The CD package

After you do remove the box's outer sleeve and open the box, you'll find enclosed a CD sleeve that contains the iPod At a Glance and User's Guides, the multilingual Limited Product Warranty booklet, and the Software License Agreement. You'll also find a CD that contains the Mac or Windows software necessary to make your iPod interact with your computer.

If you're like most people, you may glance at the At a Glance Guide and may look at the first page or two of the User's Guide but will shove the other paperwork out of the way immediately to get to the CD. Because you won't read the fine print, allow me to draw your attention to the most important points in these documents:

- **Learn more.** The User's Guide suggests that if you want to learn more about your iPod than what is presented in this slim guide, you choose iPod Help from the iTunes 2 Help menu (when you're using the Mac model) or iPod Help from MusicMatch Jukebox's Help menu (if you have the Windows model). This suggestion is a dandy and one that I heartily endorse. Although the book you hold in your hands is comprehensive, capabilities may have been added to the iPod and iTunes since this book went to print.

- **One-year warranty.** Those of you who own one of the original iPods are undoubtedly about to put down this book and send me a stern letter that begins: "Listen, Mr. Smartypants Writer, my iPod came with a 90-day warranty. Why intentionally deceive your readers?"

  To which I have to answer, "Who, me?" You see, the original iPods *did* ship with a 90-day warranty. After Apple received a significant amount of flack for offering such a skimpy warranty, however, it ever-so-quietly changed the terms of that warranty to one year on all iPods.

- **Permitted uses and restrictions.** By using the iPod and its software, you automatically agree to the Software License Agreement. When you agree to this thing, you swear that you won't use the software to copy material that you are not legally permitted to reproduce. I'll discuss the ethics of piracy later, but in the meantime, know that if you use iTunes or MusicMatch Jukebox to copy CDs that you don't own or pack your iPod with music files pirated from the Internet, you are breaking the terms of the agreement and conceivably could be called on the carpet by Apple for doing so.

- **Don't hurt yourself.** The Safety and Cleaning portion of the User's Guide suggests that you avoid performing obviously boneheaded actions with your iPod. Jamming the earbuds into the deepest recesses of your ear canals and cranking the volume could damage your hearing, for example. Operating an automobile while listening to the iPod through the earbuds could make driving less safe. Using the iPod in areas where the temperature exceeds 158 degrees Fahrenheit could break the iPod (but it likely would break you first). And taking the thing into the bathtub with you isn't such a smooth idea unless running a few thousand volts through your body is your idea of a good time.

The earbuds

Included with your iPod is a set of headphones that you place inside—rather than over—your ear (**Figure 1.1**). This style of headphones is known as *earbuds*. Two foam disks fit over the earbuds. (Apple includes two pairs of these foam disks in the box.) These disks not only grip the inside of the ear—

Figure 1.1 The iPod's earbuds and pads.

helping to keep the earbuds in place—but also make the earbuds more comfortable to wear. The hard plastic surface of the earbuds will begin to hurt after a while. And yes, the disks clearly display detritus picked up inside your ears—thus discouraging others from borrowing your headphones.

Just as you'll find a wide range of foot and head sizes among groups of people, you'll discover that the size of the opening to the ear varies among people. The earbuds included with the original iPods were a little larger than other earbuds you may have seen. Some people (including your humble author) found these headphones a little uncomfortable. The latest iPods include smaller earbuds that I find much more comfortable. With the foam disks in place, you shouldn't have trouble keeping the earbuds in place regardless of how large or small the opening to your ears is. But if you find the earbuds uncomfortable, you can purchase smaller or larger earbuds, or you can opt for a pair of over-the-ear headphones.

Regrettably, it may be difficult to find a set of earbuds that sounds as good as the set included with the iPod. Apple made great efforts to create the finest music player on the planet, and it didn't skimp on the headphones.

The included earbuds use 18mm drivers with Neodymium transducer magnets and offer a frequency range of 20 to 20,000 Hz. If you're like me, you wouldn't know a Neodymium transducer magnet if it walked up and offered to buy you lunch, but you should know that the frequency range of 20 to 20,000 Hz is what's offered by a good home stereo.

You'll find that the earbuds produce richer sound than most earbuds you're likely to stumble across and that their sound is well balanced. Without adding equalization to a song, you'll find that the sound doesn't overemphasize low or high frequencies.

The FireWire cable, power adapter, and FireWire adapter

But wait—there's more. The left half of the box contains the iPod's FireWire cable, power adapter, and—if you have the Windows version of the iPod—a FireWire 6-pin-to-4-pin cable adapter (**Figure 1.2**).

Reflecting the cohesiveness of the overall design, both the FireWire cable and power adapter come in white and are stamped with the Apple logo. The FireWire cable adapter lacks the Apple logo. There's little to say about the FireWire cable other than that it's 2 meters long and sturdy.

The power adapter sports a single FireWire port at the back and features retractable power prongs—a wonderful idea if you prefer that whatever you carry the adapter in isn't punctured by the prongs.

Figure 1.2 The FireWire cable, power adapter, and FireWire adapter (FireWire adapter included with Windows models only).

Your power adapter isn't required to charge your iPod. The iPod will charge when it's connected to a Mac or PC (though the computer has to be on and awake; a sleeping computer won't charge your iPod). But the iPod *is* a portable device, after all. And because it is, you may not have a computer with you when you want to charge it. Simple enough—just string a six-pin FireWire cable between the adapter and the iPod, and wait as long as four hours for the iPod to charge fully. (It will charge to 80 percent of battery capacity in an hour.)

Note that the power adapter is capable of handling AC input from 100 to 240 volts—meaning that with the proper adapter, you can power the iPod in countries that use the 240-volt standard without having to use a power converter.

Play Time and Battery Life

Apple claims that the iPod can play for 10 hours when fully charged. This is absolutely true—given the proper conditions.

Apple suggests that you'll squeeze the most life out of an iPod charge by playing files that are smaller than 24 MB, keeping your mitts off the Next Track and Previous Track buttons, turning off backlighting, setting the iPod's equalization settings (the controls for boosting or cutting certain audio frequencies—known as *EQ*) to None, and turning off the Sound Check option.

Files larger than 24 MB exceed the device's RAM buffer, causing the iPod to access the hard drive more often and use up the iPod's battery charge more quickly. Pushing the Next Track and Previous Track buttons likewise requires the iPod to access the hard drive more often. Slathering EQ on your tunes or evening out the volume between songs with Sound Check apparently taxes the hard drive as well. And the power necessary to light up your iPod's screen is sure to shorten play time.

The remote control

When Apple issued its new iPods in July 2002, it included—with the 10 and 20 GB models—a couple of items requested by past iPod buyers. Item No. 1 was a remote control (**Figure 1.3**).

Figure 1.3
The remote control sports Play, Pause, Fast Forward, Rewind, and Volume controls.

Unless you're planning a career as a Old West gunfighter and need to practice your quick draw, you'll find it inconvenient to reach into your pocket every time you want to adjust the iPod's volume or skip over a song that has grown tiresome. To end such wear and tear on your elbow, Apple designed a very stylish and quite functional wired remote control that plugs into the iPod's Sound Output port. (Then you plug your headphones into the headphone jack on the wired remote.) Using the remote, you can adjust volume, play or pause a song, fast-forward and rewind, and skip to the next or previous song. The remote control even has a Hold switch that locks the remote's buttons—a real boon when you don't want an accidental squeeze of the remote to ratchet up the iPod's volume. But that's not all. The remote control is designed like a clothespin to clip onto a handy piece of fabric—your pants pocket or lapel, for example.

The carrying case

Item No. 2 is Apple's iPod carrying case (**Figure 1.4**). This case is more than just a fashion statement; it's also there for your protection (or, at least, your iPod's protection). After all, the iPod is a *portable* music player, and as such, you naturally assume that it's going to get carried around. Rather than risk scratching it by placing it in a key-crammed pocket or dropping it by putting it in a shirt pocket, wouldn't it be slick if you could just clip the thing to your body in some fashion?

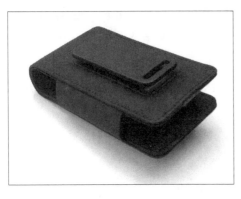

Figure 1.4 The carrying case included with the 10 and 20 GB iPods.

Apple eventually thought so too and included a case with the 10 and 20 GB models. The included case is far from my favorite (to learn about cases on which I'm keener, see Chapter 7). Why? You can't access the iPod's front controls without removing the iPod from the case, the belt clip is delicate and will break with the tiniest bit of rough treatment, and the case doesn't offer much cushioning (a vital feature if you drop the thing when it's full of iPod).

On the other hand, Apple's not making a ton of money on the case and remote control. The old 10 GB iPod cost $499 without a case. The latest 20 GB iPod costs $499 with a case and remote control. If you look at it the right way, Apple's really giving you a *free* case and remote control—a darned bargain.

The iPod

And, of course, there's the iPod itself.

Now that you own it, you're welcome to remove the iPod from the box, strip away the protective plastic sheeting, and ignore or admire the admonition printed on the plastic: *Don't steal music.*

The first thing you'll likely notice is that the iPod is even more lovely than it appears in the magazine ads and on the Web and TV. The second thing is that it's more solidly built and heavier than you imagined. At 4.02 inches tall, 2.43 inches wide, and 0.78 inch thick (the 10 GB and 20 GB models are a bit thicker at 0.72 and 0.84 inch thick, respectively), the iPod will take you a bit aback when you heft all 6.5 ounces of it (or 7.2 ounces of it, if you have the 20 GB model). It's not a brick by any means. But the stainless-steel back and dual-plastic top casing add some weight to the device.

It's also easier to smudge than you might have guessed. The ultrareflective back plate is a visual delight, but the second you touch your iPod, fingerprints and smudges will mar its surface. If such smears and smudges bother you, carry a soft eyeglass cleaning cloth, and buff the back whenever the mood strikes.

Not so obvious are what lurks within the iPod and what the device can do. I'll clear up the mystery.

Capacity

As this book goes to press, Apple offers three iPod models: one with a 5 GB hard drive, another with a 10 GB drive, and a third with a 20 GB drive. Other than that—and the bundled accessories (the case and remote control)—there's no apparent difference among the three models.

The hard-drive capacity is a bit deceiving. The drives technically hold 5 GB, 10 GB, and 20 GB, respectively, but after they're formatted, you'll find that the 5 GB drive actually holds 4.6 GB of data, the 10 GB model holds 9.2 GB, and the 20 GB holds 18.5 GB. The reason for the discrepancy is that Apple and hard-drive manufacturers measure megabytes differently. Drive manufacturers maintain that 1 MB equals 1 million bytes (1,000 x 1,000 bytes). Apple claims that a megabyte is actually 1,048,576 bytes (1,024 x 1,024 bytes). So this difference is really a difference in semantics. The drive manufacturer and Apple agree that a 5 GB drive is a 5 GB drive. It's just that the Mac and iPod OS show that such a drive actually holds less information if you use Apple's definition of a megabyte.

Regardless of how megabytes are calculated, you do lose a portion of the hard drive's space. The iPod can't run without an operating system, and that operating system takes up some space. Also, when the drive is formatted, a small portion of the hard drive is reserved for internal chores.

Is the possible loss of 0.4, 0.8, and 1.5 GB something to lose sleep over? Hardly. You have plenty of room to store files. The 5 GB model, for example, can hold 1,000 four-minute MP3 songs encoded at 160 kilobits (kbps) per second—more than 66 hours of music. I'll discuss kilobits and music encoding elsewhere in the book, but for the time being, you should know that this 160 kbps rate is reasonably high, producing files that sound remarkably good. Many MP3 files that you'll find on the Web are encoded at the lower rate of 128 kbps. If you were to store nothing but MP3 files encoded at 128 kbps on your iPod, you'd be able to play 1,243 tunes on your 5 GB iPod without hearing the same one twice (more than 84 hours of music). Double these numbers for the 10 GB model, and quadruple them for the 20 GB iPod (that's 11 full days of music).

Skip protection

The iPod sports a 32 MB DRAM (Dynamic RAM) memory buffer. When the iPod moves music from the hard drive to your ears, it loads into that buffer about 20 minutes of music (if you're playing an MP3 file encoded at 160 kbps). After shoveling the music into the buffer, the hard drive spins down, saving wear and tear on both the drive and the iPod's battery.

This scheme also allows 20 minutes of skip-free music playback. Yes, for nearly 20 minutes, you can jump, jive, and wail, listening to your music with nary a glitch. The iPod will skip only when data is being moved off the hard drive and into the buffer.

If you've never owned another MP3 player, you might not realize how impressive this feature is. Lesser players offer skip protection that's measured in seconds rather than minutes.

Supported audio formats

Although the iPod is usually referred to as an MP3 player, it can actually play music encoded in a few formats. MP3 is the most desirable because (as I explained in the introduction) thanks to their relatively small sizes, you can jam a lot of MP3 files into the iPod.

But the iPod also allows you to play AIFF (Audio Interchange File Format, the kind of files used on audio CDs) and WAV files (the Microsoft Windows audio format). Because they're not compressed, AIFF and WAV files are of higher quality than MP3 files. But MP3 files encoded at 320 Kbps—the maximum resolution allowed for MP3 files on the iPod—sound amazingly good.

The tradeoff is that these files consume 10 MB per minute of stereo music. Using AIFF and WAV files means not only giving up a lot of hard drive space for fewer files (you can fit about

115 four-minute AIFF files on a 5 GB iPod), but also draining the RAM buffer much more quickly. This situation causes the hard drive to kick in more often and the battery to drain more rapidly. Also, because of the files' size, moving AIFF and WAV songs from your Mac to the iPod takes longer than moving the same number of MP3 files.

> *As this edition goes to press, MPEG-4 audio files are not supported on the iPod—though they are in Apple's Quick-Time technology and iTunes application. MPEG-4 audio files are even smaller than MP3 files—around 7% of the original file's size—and sound better than MP3. (Over computer speakers, it's very difficult to tell the difference between an MPEG-4 and the original, uncompressed song.) I wouldn't be terribly surprised if, before the next edition of this book ships, the iPod also supports the MPEG-4 standard.*

What's the Difference?

The iPod comes in two flavors: the original iPod for Macintosh and the new iPod for Windows. Is there a difference between the two besides the outer packaging?

Absolutely.

To begin with, the iPod for Windows model includes a 6-to-4-pin FireWire adapter. This adapter is necessary because some PCs ship with the smaller variety of FireWire port used on many of today's digital camcorders. Rather than create a separate cable for Windows users, Apple includes a standard 6-pin-to-6-pin FireWire cable with all its iPods and flings this adapter into the iPod for Windows box for the convenience of its PC-using customers.

The software is also different. With the Mac version of the iPod, you move music on and off your iPod via Apple's iTunes music player/encoder application. There is no version of iTunes for Windows. Rather than create one, Apple cut a deal with MusicMatch (**www.musicmatch.com**) to make that company's MusicMatch Jukebox music player/encoder application compatible with the Windows version of the iPod. I'll discuss the specifics of both these programs in Chapters 2 and 3.

The way that the hard drive is formatted is different as well. The Macintosh model's hard drive is formatted as a Mac OS Extended (HFS+) volume—the same kind of formatting used by default on the Macintosh. The Windows iPod's hard drive uses FAT32 formatting—the native formatting scheme for Windows.

continues on next page

What's the Difference? *continued*

Windows PCs can't recognize a Mac OS Extended volume natively, so should you plug your Mac iPod into a PC, the PC wouldn't recognize the iPod. The Mac, however, can recognize FAT32 volumes. If you plug your Windows iPod into a Mac, the Mac will treat it almost exactly like a Macintosh iPod. Just as you can with a Macintosh iPod, you can use iTunes to move music to the iPod, as well as add calendars and contacts to the device. The only thing you can't do with a Windows iPod is install a Macintosh operating system on it and then boot from the iPod.

Finally, the capabilities of the two versions are different. Although the Windows version of the iPod emulates most of the features of the Mac version—music playback, multiple ways to browse your playlists, and calendar and contact functions—the Mac version has a few features that are not available in the Windows iPod. These features include:

- The ability to play Audible.com content.

- The Sound Check option, which makes playback volume consistent among songs. (The MusicMatch Jukebox software offers a similar feature, but all processing is done on the PC before the files are exported to the iPod.)

- The ability to browse by Composer.

- Play counts, a feature that keeps track of the number of times you've played a song.

- Play dates, a feature that keeps track of recently played songs.

- Ratings. In iTunes 3, you can rate a song from one to five stars.

- Per-song EQ settings.

- Smart playlists, a feature that allows you to create playlists based on such criteria as rating and style (your highest-rated easy-listening songs, for example).

Controls

The iPod has rightly been praised for its ease of use. As with all its products, Apple strove to make the iPod as intuitive as possible, placing a limited number of controls and ports on the device. When you offer such a limited set of controls, of course, some have to perform more than one function. In the following pages, I examine just what these controls and ports do.

On the face of it

On the front of your iPod (**Figure 1.5**), you'll find a display and set of navigation controls arrayed in a wheel. Here's what they do and how they work.

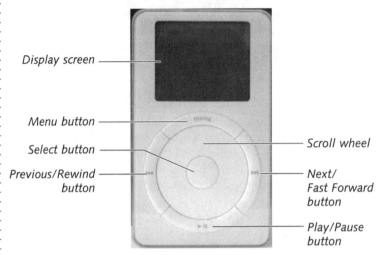

Figure 1.5 The iPod's display and navigation controls.

The display

Near the top of the device, the iPod sports a 2-inch-diagonal, monochrome liquid crystal display with a resolution of 160 by 128 pixels. You can turn on backlighting (switch on a light that makes the display easier to read in low-light situations) by holding down the Menu button.

Play/Pause button

If you scan the surface of your iPod, you'll notice that it bears no recognizable On/Off switch. That job is handled by the Play/Pause button—the button that occupies the bottom of the iPod control wheel. Just press this button to switch the iPod on, and hold it down for about three seconds to switch the iPod off.

As its name hints, this button is the one you push to play or pause the highlighted song.

Previous/Rewind button

Press this button once to go to the previous song in the playlist; hold it down to rewind through a song. When you rewind or fast-forward through a song, you move in small increments at first. As you continue to hold the button down, you move in larger increments.

Next/Fast Forward button

Press this button once to go to the next song in the playlist; hold it down to fast-forward through a song. When you rewind or fast-forward through a song, you move in small increments at first. As you continue to hold the button down, you move in larger increments.

Menu button

Pressing the Menu button takes you back through the interface the way you came. If you've moved from the main iPod screen to the Browse screen, for example, and you press the Menu button, you'll move back to the main iPod screen. If you've moved from the main iPod screen through the Playlist screen to a particular song within a particular playlist, each time you press the Menu button, you'll move back one screen.

Holding the Menu button down for about two seconds turns backlighting on or off.

Scroll wheel

Inside the aforementioned ring of buttons is the scroll wheel. On the original 5 and 10 GB iPods, this scroll wheel turned; on current models, it doesn't. Rather, the scroll wheel is stationary and touch-sensitive. Move your thumb across it to "scroll" the wheel.

Moving the wheel (or, in the case of the new iPods, your thumb) clockwise highlights items below the selected item; moving the wheel counterclockwise highlights items above the selected item. If a window is larger than the display, moving the scroll wheel will cause the window to scroll up or down when the first or last item in the list is highlighted.

You also use the scroll wheel to adjust volume and move to a particular location in a song.

The iPod includes a feature that allows you to hear a click as you use the scroll wheel. This wonderful feature provides you aural feedback on how quickly you're spinning the wheel.

Select button

The bull's-eye of the iPod—the center button—selects a menu item. If the Settings menu item is selected, for example, pushing the Select button moves you to the Settings screen, where you can select additional settings.

When you press the Select button while a song is playing and the Play screen is visible, you move to another Play screen, where you can *scrub* (quickly navigate forward and back with the scroll wheel) your song.

Up top

The top of the iPod (**Figure 1.6**) carries two ports and one switch. Here's what they do.

Figure 1.6
The iPod's FireWire port, Headphones port, and Hold switch.

FireWire port

As the name implies, this port is where you plug in your six-pin FireWire cable. The iPod uses the FireWire cable both for power (power pulled from either an up-and-running-but-not-sleeping computer or the power adapter) and for transferring data between the iPod and a Mac or PC. The latest iPod models include a plastic cover that keeps gunk out of the FireWire port. The original iPods lack this cover.

Headphones port

When the iPod was first released, a few people were concerned that it bore only a single audio-out port: the Headphones port. Other, less-capable music players carried two ports: one for headphones and another for *line-level* output, which is the kind of output that's acceptable to home and car stereos.

It turned out that there was no need for concern. Of course you can plug a set of headphones into the iPod, and yes, you can use any set of headphones as long as it carries a stereo Walkman-style miniplug. But you can also plug the iPod into your stereo. Elsewhere in the book, I'll explain how to do so. For those of you who are interested in such numbers, the iPod has a maximum output power of 60mW rms (30mW per channel) everywhere except in France.

> *No, I'm not kidding. The default output of the iPod exceeds the decibel limit allowed for consumer audio devices in France. Apple has issued an update that limits the iPod's audio output to levels acceptable to the French government.*

Hold switch

When you push the Hold switch to the left, the front buttons lock. This feature is particularly handy when you don't want the iPod to begin playing when it's bumped in your backpack or pushed in your pocket.

Interface

Considering how easy the iPod is to use, it's hard to believe the number of navigation screens that make up its interface. In the following pages, I scrutinize each screen.

Main screen

The main screen (**Figure 1.7**), which displays the word *iPod* at the top, is your gateway to the iPod. In a way, it's akin to the Mac's Finder or Windows' My Computer window—a place to get started. In the main screen on an iPod running iPod Update 1.2 or later you can select the following items:

- Playlists
- Browse
- Extras
- Settings
- About
- Now Playing (if a song is playing or paused)

Figure 1.7
The iPod's
Main screen.

Here's what you'll find within each item.

Playlists

When you choose Playlists (**Figure 1.8**) and press the Select button, you'll see a screen that contains the playlists that you have downloaded to your iPod. These playlists are created and configured in iTunes on a Macintosh and MusicMatch Jukebox on a Windows PC. How you configure them is up to you. You may, for example, want to gather all your jazz favorites in one playlist and put ska in another. Or, if you have an iPod shared by the family, Dad may gather his psychedelic songs of the '60s in his personal playlist, while sister Sue creates a playlist full of hip-hop and house music. When I discuss iTunes and MusicMatch Jukebox in later chapters, I'll look at other approaches for putting together playlists.

Figure 1.8
The Playlists screen.

You may notice a couple of other playlists that you didn't create: 60's Music, My Top Rated, Recently Played, and Top 25 Most Played, for example. These playlists are new to the Macintosh version of the iPod (they're not found on the Windows version of the iPod—see the discussion of Smart Playlists in Chapter 2 to find out why) and, as their names hint, list songs recorded in the '60s, songs that you think are just swell, songs that you've played in the not-too-distant past, and songs that you've played more often than others. Later in the book, I'll describe what makes these playlists tick.

After you select a playlist and press the Select button, the songs within that playlist appear in a scrollable screen (**Figure 1.9**), and the name of the playlist appears at the top of the screen. Just select the song you want to play, and press the Select button. When you do, you'll move to the Play screen (**Figure 1.10**), which can display the number of songs in the playlist, the name of the playing song, the artist, and the name of the album from which the song came. (If some of this information didn't appear in iTunes or MusicMatch Jukebox originally, it won't be displayed on your iPod.) Also appearing in this screen are two timer displays: elapsed time and remaining time. The screen contains a graphic thermometer display that gives you a visual representation of how far along you are in the song.

Figure 1.9 The songs within a playlist.

Figure 1.10 The Play screen.

You can move one more screen from the Play screen by using the scroll wheel or Select button. If you turn the scroll wheel, you'll move to a screen nearly identical to the Play screen where you can adjust the iPod's volume (**Figure 1.11**). When you stop moving the scroll wheel, you'll be taken back to the Play screen after a couple of seconds. If you press the Select button while you're in the Play screen, you'll be able to scrub through the song (**Figure 1.12**). Like the Play screen, the Scrub screen carries a thermometer display that indicates the playing location with a small diamond. Just push the scroll wheel back or forth to start scrubbing.

Figure 1.11 The Play screen's volume control.

Figure 1.12 The Play screen's scrub control.

Browse

With the release of iPod Update 1.2, the iPod allows you to browse the contents of your portable player in several ways: by Artist, Album, Songs, Genres, and Composers. When you highlight the Browse selection in the iPod's main window and press the Select button, you'll find all these choices listed in the Browse window. Here's what you'll find for each entry.

Artists

The Artists screen displays the names of any artists on your iPod (**Figure 1.13**). Choose an artist's name and press Select, and you'll be transported to that artist's screen, where you have the opportunity to play every song on your iPod by that artist or select a particular album by that artist.

Figure 1.13
The Artists screen.

You'll also spy the All entry at the top of the Artists screen. Should you choose this entry, you'll be taken to the All Albums screen, where you can select all albums by all artists. The All Albums screen contains an All command of its own. Select this command, and you'll move to the All Songs screen, which lists all songs by all artists on your iPod. (But if a song doesn't have an artist entry, the song won't appear in this screen.)

Albums

Choose the Albums entry and press Select, and you'll see every album on your iPod (**Figure 1.14**). Choose an album and press the Select button to play the album from beginning to end. The Albums screen also contains an All button, which, when selected, displays all the songs on all the albums on your iPod. (If the song doesn't have an album entry, it won't appear in this screen.)

Figure 1.14
The Albums screen.

An album entry can contain a single song. As long as the album field has been filled in for a particular song within iTunes or MusicMatch Jukebox (I'll discuss this topic in Chapters 2 and 3), that song will appear in the Albums screen.

Songs

Choose Songs and press Select, and you'll be presented with a list of all the songs on your iPod (**Figure 1.15**).

Figure 1.15
The Songs screen.

Genres

The iPod has the ability to sort songs by genre: Acoustic, Blues, Reggae, and Techno, for example. If a song has been tagged with a genre entry (see the sidebar "I'll Need to See Some ID" in this section), you can choose it by genre in the Genres screen (**Figure 1.16**).

Figure 1.16
The Genres screen.

Composers

The iPod can also group songs by composers. This feature, added in the iPod Update 1.2, allows you to sort classical music more easily (**Figure 1.17**).

Figure 1.17
The Composers screen.

I'll Need to See Some ID

You're undoubtedly wondering how the iPod knows that Bob Marley's "Buffalo Soldier" is reggae and Paul Hindemith composed *Mathis der Maler*. There's no profound trick to it. The iPod simply looks at each file's *ID3 tags*. ID3 tags are little bits of information that are included with a song's music data, such as title, album, artist, composer, genre, and year the song was recorded.

If someone has taken the time to enter this information (someone like you, for example), the iPod will use it to sort songs by genre, composer, or decade recorded. You can edit a song's ID3 tag in iTunes and MusicMatch Jukebox. In Chapters 2 and 3, I'll show you how.

Extras

The Extras screen is the means to all the iPod's nonmusical functions—its contacts, calendars, clock, and game. Here's what you'll find for each entry.

Contacts

The capability for the iPod to store and view contacts was introduced in the iPod Software 1.1 Updater. I'll discuss how to create contacts elsewhere in the book. In the meantime, you need know only that to access your contacts, you choose Contacts in the Extras screen and press the Select button (**Figure 1.18**). Scroll through your list of contacts and press Select again to view the information within a contact. If a contact contains more information than will fit in the display, use the scroll wheel to scroll down the window.

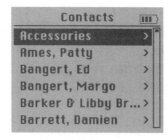

Figure 1.18
The Contacts screen.

Calendar

The ability for the iPod to list your appointments came with version 1.2 of the iPod software. I'll address calendar creation later in the book, so for now, just know that when you click the Calendar entry, you'll see the current month displayed in a window with the current day highlighted (**Figure 1.19**). If a day has an event attached to it, that day displays a small black rectangle. Use the scroll wheel to move to a different day—scroll forward to look into the future, and scroll back to be transported back in time. When you want to see the details of an event, scroll to its day, and press the Select key. The details of that event will be displayed in the resulting screen.

Clock

Yes, the iPod can tell time (that is, if you tell your iPod what time to tell in the Settings section of the device; see "Date & Time" later in this chapter). Clicking Clock displays the current time and date (**Figure 1.20**).

Figure 1.19 The Calendar screen.

Figure 1.20 The Clock screen.

Game

Once upon a time, the iPod had a hidden game that could be accessed only if you held down the Select button for several seconds in a particular screen. With the iPod Update 1.2, Apple decided to reveal this secret game (**Figure 1.21**). When you choose and select the Game option in the Extras screen, you'll be taken to this breakout-style game. Use the Select button to begin playing and the scroll wheel to move the paddle.

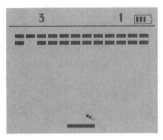

Figure 1.21
Get into the game.

Settings

The Settings screen (**Figure 1.22**) is the path to your iPod preferences—including contrast and startup-volume settings, EQ selection, and the language the iPod displays. The following sections look at each setting individually.

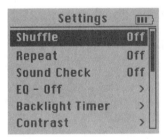

Figure 1.22
The Settings screen.

Shuffle

Selecting Shuffle and pressing the Select button toggles you through three settings: Off, Songs, and Albums. When it's set to Off, the iPod will play the songs in a playlist in the order in which they appear onscreen. The Songs setting plays all the songs within a selected playlist or album in random order. If no album or playlist is selected, the iPod plays all the songs on the iPod in random order. And the Albums setting plays the songs within each album in order but shuffles the order in which the albums are played.

Repeat

The Repeat setting also offers three options: Off, One, and All. When you select Off, the iPod won't repeat songs. Select One, and you'll hear the selected song play repeatedly. Select All, and all the songs within the selected playlist or album will be repeated when the playlist or album has played all the way through. If you haven't selected a playlist or album, all the songs on the iPod will repeat after they've played through.

Sound Check

New with the iPod Update 1.2, Sound Check is a feature that attempts to maintain a consistent volume among songs. Before Sound Check arrived on the scene, you'd constantly fiddle with the iPod's volume because one song was too loud, the next too quiet, the next quieter still, and the next painfully loud. Sound Check does its best to produce volumes that don't vary so wildly.

To use Sound Check, you must first select the Sound Check option in iTunes 3 (iTunes 2, the version of iTunes that's compatible with Mac OS 9, doesn't carry the Sound Check feature), have iTunes 3 apply Sound Check to the music files on your computer, and then download those Sound Checked files to your iPod.

> *iPod for Windows users may be concerned that I haven't mentioned how Sound Check works with their iPod model. It doesn't. Sound Check is exclusively an iTunes/iPod for Mac feature. However, MusicMatch Jukebox includes a feature called Volume Leveling that does much the same thing as Sound Check. The difference is that once you've processed songs with Volume Leveling on the PC and then transferred them to your iPod, you can't turn the Volume Leveling feature off on the iPod. I'll discuss Volume Leveling in greater detail in Chapter 3.*

EQ

Ever since the 1.1 software update, you've been able to assign specific *equalization* (EQ) settings to your iPod. And what, exactly, is equalization? It's the process of boosting or cutting certain frequencies in the audio spectrum—making the low frequencies louder and the high frequencies quieter, for example. If you've ever adjusted the bass and treble controls on your home or car stereo, you get the idea.

The iPod now comes with the same EQ settings as iTunes 2. Those settings include:

- Off
- Acoustic
- Bass Booster
- Bass Reducer
- Classical
- Dance
- Deep
- Electronic
- Flat
- Hip Hop
- Jazz
- Latin
- Lounge
- Piano
- Pop
- R & B
- Rock
- Small Speakers
- Spoken Word
- Treble Booster
- Treble Reducer
- Vocal Booster

Although you can listen to each EQ setting to get an idea of what it does, if you're using a Mac, you may find it easier to open iTunes; choose Equalizer from the Window menu; and, in the resulting Equalizer window, choose the various EQ settings from the window's pop-up menu. The equalizer's 10-band sliders will show you which frequencies have been boosted and which have been cut. Any slider that appears above the 0 dB line indicates a frequency that has been boosted. Conversely, sliders that appear below 0 dB have been cut.

MusicMatch Jukebox also includes an equalizer feature, but it's not compatible with the iPod's equalizer settings. If you want to use EQ with the Windows version of the iPod, you must configure EQ settings on the iPod manually (see the sidebar "EQ and the iPod" in this section for details).

I'll look at the equalizer in greater depth when I examine iTunes and MusicMatch Jukebox.

EQ and the iPod

Apple was kind enough to include a configurable equalizer (EQ) as part of the iPod Software 1.1 Updater, but the way that the EQ settings in iTunes and the iPod interact is a little confusing. Allow me to end that confusion.

Macintosh. Mac users undoubtedly know that in iTunes 2 and iTunes 3, you can assign an EQ setting to songs individually by clicking the song, pressing Command-I, clicking the Options tab, and then choosing an EQ setting from the Equalizer Preset menu. When you move songs to your iPod, these EQ settings move right along with them, but you won't be able to use them unless you configure the iPod correctly.

If, for example, you have EQ switched off on the iPod, songs that have an assigned EQ preset won't play with that setting. Instead, your songs will play without the benefit of EQ. If you set the iPod's EQ to Flat, the EQ setting that you preset in iTunes will play on the iPod. If you select one of the other EQ settings on the iPod (Latin or Electronic, for example), songs without EQ presets assigned in iTunes will use the iPod EQ setting. Songs with EQ settings assigned in iTunes will use the iTunes setting.

If you'd like to hear how a particular song sounds on your iPod with a different EQ setting, start playing the song on the iPod, press the Menu button until you return to the Main screen, select Settings, select EQ, and then select one of the EQ settings. The song will immediately take on the EQ setting you've chosen, but this setting won't stick on subsequent playback. If you want to change the song's EQ more permanently, you must do so in iTunes.

Windows. I'm afraid that this is another instance where the Mac version of the iPod has an advantage over the Windows version. Although MusicMatch Jukebox includes an equalization feature, it isn't compatible with the iPod. Although you can use EQ within MusicMatch Jukebox, those EQ settings won't be copied to your iPod, as they are with the Mac version of the iPod. To change the EQ on your iPod, you must follow the method I mentioned earlier: switch to the EQ setting you want in the Settings screen while the iPod is playing.

Backlight Timer

The iPod's backlight pulls its power from the battery, and when it's left on for very long, you significantly shorten the amount of time you can play your iPod on a single charge. For this reason, Apple includes a backlight timer that automatically switches off backlighting after a certain user-configurable interval. You set that interval by choosing the Backlight Timer setting.

Settings available to you are Off, 1 Second, 2 Seconds, 5 Seconds, 10 Seconds, and (for those who give not a whit about battery life) Always On.

Contrast

To change the display's contrast, select the Contrast setting, press Select, and use the scroll wheel to darken or lighten the display.

Alarms

New to the iPod is the capability to send up an alert when a calendar event has an alarm attached to it. The three settings are Off (no alarm is issued), On (a little tinkling sound erupts from the iPod—the iPod itself, not through the headphones—and an alarm screen that describes the event is displayed), and Silent (the alarm screen appears without audio accompaniment).

Sleep Timer

To save battery power, the iPod includes a sleep function that powers down your iPod after a certain time has elapsed. The Sleep Timer settings allows you to determine how long an interval of inactivity has to pass before your iPod takes a snooze. The available settings are Off, 15 Minutes, 30 Minutes, 60 Minutes, 90 Minutes, and 120 Minutes.

Date & Time

The iPod also tells time. Choose Date & Time in the Settings window and press Select to access commands for setting your time zone (time zones include listings for Standard Time as well as Daylight Saving Time) and for entering the current time and date.

Contacts

The Contacts setting allows you to sort your contacts by last or first name and to display those contacts by last or first name.

Clicker

The simple On or Off setting allows you to turn off the click that iPod makes when you press a button or move your thumb across the scroll wheel.

Language

The iPod can display 15 languages, including English, Japanese, French, German, Spanish, Italian, Danish, Norwegian, Swedish, Portuguese, and Chinese. In some instances, the iPod can display multiple languages. It's possible to view American titles on an iPod that displays the Japanese language, for example. I'll show you how when I talk about iTunes.

> *Should someone set your iPod to a language you don't understand—one of my favorite April Fool's jokes, by the way—you can reset it by choosing the fourth command from the top in the Main menu, choosing the third menu from the bottom in the next screen, and finally selecting your language in the resulting list.*

Legal

If you care to view a few copyright notices, feel free to choose the Legal setting and press the Select button.

Reset All Settings

As the name implies, selecting Reset All Settings, pressing the Select button, and selecting Reset returns the iPod to its default settings. This doesn't mean that your music library will be erased. Rather, this setting turns Shuffle off, Repeat off, Sound Check off, EQ off, Backlight Timer off, Contrast to the middle setting, Alarms on, Sleep Timer off, Clicker on, and Language to English (though this setup may be different on iPods sold in non-English-speaking countries).

About

The About screen is where you'll find the name of your iPod (changeable within iTunes), the number of songs the iPod currently holds, the total hard-drive space (4.6 GB for the 5 GB model, 9.2 GB for the 10 GB iPod, and 18.5 GB for the 20 GB model), the amount of available free space, the software version, and your iPod's serial number. If you have the Windows iPod, you'll also see the Format Windows entry. (The Mac version of the iPod doesn't bother to tell you that it's formatted for the Macintosh.)

Managing
Music with the
Macintosh

A high-performance automobile is little more than an interesting amalgam of metal and plastic if it's missing tires and fuel. Sure, given the proper slope (and, perhaps, a helpful tailwind), that car is capable of movement, but the resulting journey leaves much to be desired. So, too, the iPod is a less-capable music-making vehicle without Apple's music player/encoder, iTunes. The two—like coffee and cream, dill and pickle, and Fred and Ginger—were simply meant for each other.

This chapter isn't intended to take the place of a full-featured guide to iTunes, such as my buddy Bob LeVitus' *Little iTunes Book* (Peachpit Press, 2002). But to best understand what makes the iPod's world turn, you must be familiar with how it and iTunes work together to move music on and off your iPod. In the following pages, you'll learn just that.

iTunes, uTunes, We All Croon for iTunes

Released in January 2001, iTunes was Apple's second "i" application. (The first was the digital video-editing application iMovie.) Like Casady & Greene's SoundJam, iTunes was capable of playing and encoding MP3 files on a Macintosh. It featured a simple interface that allowed users to turn audio CDs into MP3 files easily, drag and drop songs between the Library (a master list of all the songs on your Mac) and user-created playlists, and record (or *burn*) customized audio CDs from within the application.

When Apple unveiled the first iPod, it also took the wraps off iTunes 2: an enhanced version of iTunes that, in addition to providing the means for moving music from the Mac to the iPod, introduced a 10-band graphic equalizer (EQ) with 22 presets, a sound enhancer that brings a livelier sound to tunes played in the application, and the ability to fade tracks played in iTunes into one another. (As we go to press, sound enhancement and fades don't transfer to the iPod.)

To accompany its release of new iPod models in July 2002, Apple issued iTunes 3, a Mac OS X-only version of iTunes that includes such enhancements as the Sound Check feature, support for playing back Audible.com spoken-word files, the capability to rate songs, and support for smart playlists—playlists you create based on such factors as rating, the number of times you've played a track, and style. Mac users who continue to run Mac OS 9 can still download music to their iPods with iTunes 2 but won't be able to take advantage of these new features.

Where necessary, I identify iTunes 2 and iTunes 3 by their version numbers. If a feature works in both programs, I refer simply to iTunes. The original iTunes (which sports no version number) doesn't support the iPod and, therefore, is not terribly useful for the purposes of this book.

As I stated earlier, this chapter isn't intended to show you every shining surface of iTunes, but it will help you get familiar with the basics: encoding (or *ripping*) an audio CD with iTunes, configuring a playlist, and moving that musical material to the iPod.

Ripping a CD

Apple intended this process to be painless, and it is. Here's how to proceed:

1. Launch iTunes.

2. Insert an audio CD into your Mac's CD player/recorder.

   By default, iTunes will try to identify the CD you've inserted and log onto the Web to download the CD's song titles. This feature is very handy for those who find typing such minutia to be tedious, but if you'd prefer that this didn't happen, choose Preferences (in the iTunes menu in OS X and in the Edit menu in OS 9.2 and earlier), click the General tab, and uncheck the Connect to Internet When Needed check box (**Figure 2.1**).

Figure 2.1 To download song titles from a CD automatically, make sure that the Connect to Internet When Needed option is selected in the iTunes Preferences dialog box.

The CD will appear in iTunes' Source list and the titles in the Song list to the right (**Figure 2.2**).

Figure 2.2 This album's song titles were downloaded from the Web automatically by iTunes.

3. To convert the audio tracks to MP3 files, click the Import button (**Figure 2.3**) in the top-right corner of the iTunes window.

(To import only certain songs, choose Select None from the Edit menu and then click the box next to the songs you want to import. Click the Import button to import just those selected songs.)

iTunes will begin encoding the files.

Figure 2.3
Click this button to import CD tracks into iTunes.

*iTunes will import songs via the encoder you've chosen in the Importing tab of the iTunes Preferences dialog box (**Figure 2.4**). By default, iTunes imports songs as MP3 files, but it can also import songs as AIFF and WAV files. For more information on setting importing preferences, see the sidebar "Import Business: File Formats and Bit Rates" in this section.*

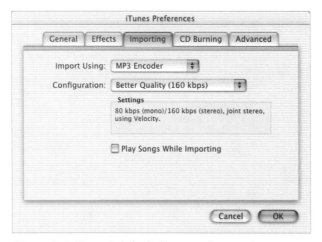

Figure 2.4 iTunes' default file-encoding settings.

4. Click the Library button.

You'll see the songs you just imported.

5. To listen to a song, click its name in the list and then click the Play button or press the spacebar.

The Unrippable Disc

There's no question that the practice of "sharing" music on the Internet has given the music industry a bad case of the jim-jams. These industry folk seem (quite reasonably) to believe that if people give music away for free, far fewer dollars will flutter into music-company coffers.

The music industry is attempting to stem the flow of music piracy by several means, including lobbying our elected officials to enact legislation that gives the music industry broad powers to protect its assets, selling older material at more reasonable prices, and making CDs difficult to copy. I'd like to address that last item here.

Sony has created discs that cannot be copied easily. Although these discs look like CDs, technically, they're not; they don't adhere to the CD standard and, therefore, cannot be labeled as CDs. When you insert one of these things into your computer's media drive, not only will the disc not play, but you also might have a dickens of a time getting it out. These discs have been known to lock up a computer's CD drive.

Fortunately, the music industry is now required to label these dangerous discs as a hazard to your computer. Should you encounter one of these things, do not attempt to play it on your Macintosh or PC. Better yet, refrain from purchasing such tainted goods. If the music industry understands that customers will stay away from these loathsome discs, it may stop making them.

Import Business: File Formats and Bit Rates

iTunes' default settings—importing audio CDs as MP3 files encoded at 160 kbps—are a good choice for your iPod, but you have the option to change them. To do so, choose Preferences (located in the Apple menu in OS X and in the Edit menu in OS 9.2 and earlier), and click the Importing tab (or the Importing button, in the case of iTunes 3) in the resulting iTunes Preferences dialog box.

The Import Using pop-up menu allows you to choose to import files in MP3, AIFF, or WAV format. As I explained earlier, MP3 files are smaller than AIFF or WAV files but don't have the same fidelity of these much-larger files. The iPod can play files encoded in any of these formats.

The Configuration pop-up menu is where you choose the resolution of the MP3 files encoded by iTunes. The default settings (**Figure 2.5**) include Good Quality (128 kbps), Better Quality (160 kbps), and High Quality (192 kbps). Files encoded with a higher bit rate sound better than those encoded at low bit rates (such as 128 kbps). But files encoded at higher bit rates also take up more space on your hard drive and iPod. If you don't care to use one of these settings, choose Custom from this same pop-up menu. In the MP3 Encoder dialog box that appears, you have the option to choose a bit rate from 8 to 320 kbps.

You can change other settings in the MP3 Encoder dialog box. By choosing the Use Variable Bit Rate Encoding (VBR) option, for example, you might produce better-sounding MP3 files (though they may be larger than if you hadn't chosen this option). You can also change the number of channels (mono or stereo) and stereo mode. For most people, the default settings work perfectly well.

It's up to you to balance quantity and quality. If you want to cram as many songs as possible onto your iPod and have what less-sensitive souls disparagingly term a "tin ear," feel free to use a low bit rate, such as 128 kbps. But unless you're listening to anything but narration (a "Books on Tape" kind of recording, for example), don't venture below 128 kbps unless you *really* don't care about quality. And marching much above 192 kbps—particularly if you're listening over headphones or computer speakers—is mostly a waste of time for all but those who have the most discerning ears.

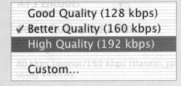

Figure 2.5
Three easy-to-choose encoding bit rates.

Songs from the Web

There's no getting around it; you can download music files from the Web easily from such legal sources as the Internet Underground Music Archives (*www.iuma.com*) and MP3.com (*www.mp3.com*), as well as from such far-from-legal sources as Internet newsgroups and HotLine servers, and via a variety of file-sharing clients. Let's put aside the legal and ethical arguments for now (I assure you that I'll address these important issues later in the book) and focus on getting music from the Web onto your iPod.

Legal Music File Sources

Despite much of what you've heard about music file sharing on the Web, there are places to get perfectly legal MP3 files. Some sites offer this music to expose unsigned bands; others give you a taste of an album in the hope that you'll purchase the CD. Such sources include:

- Internet Underground Music Archives (**www.iuma.com**)
- MP3.com (**www.mp3.com**)
- Epitonic.com (**www.epitonic.com**)
- RollingStone.com (**www.rollingstone.com**)
- Billboard.com (**www.billboard.com**)
- Amazon.com (**www.amazon.com**)
- Garageband.com (**www.garageband.com**)

If you're looking for legal live recordings of such bands as the Grateful Dead, take a look at FurthurNET (**http://furthurnet.com**). This OS X-only Java application is a peer-to-peer file-sharing service that allows users to share live recordings among themselves. Note that many of the files shared on FurthurNET are of complete shows and can take up hundreds of megabytes of storage. Use such a service only if you have a fast broadband connection and lots of room to store files.

Managing file types

Remember, the iPod is capable of playing only MP3, AIFF, and WAV files. Other audio formats exist on the Web, but these file formats are not supported by the iPod. MPEG-4-encoded audio files, which will play in Apple's QuickTime Player 6.0 and iTunes 3 (if you have QuickTime 6.0 installed), won't work on your iPod. Neither will Ogg Vorbis-encoded files. (Ogg Vorbis is a music encoder popular in the Linux world.)

If you'd like to use some other variety of audio file, you must convert it before you can bring it into iTunes. Norman Franke's free SoundApp application (**Figure 2.6;** *www.spies.com/ ~franke/SoundApp*) is a terrific utility for converting files to a form acceptable to the iPod. You may have to convert a file to the AIFF format and then convert it to MP3 within iTunes.

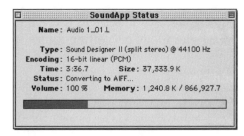

Figure 2.6
SoundApp can convert a multitude of audio file types.

Note, however, that you may never be able to convert certain types of files. RealAudio files, for example, are generally streamed from the Web (meaning that the audio file is stored somewhere on the Web and played like a radio broadcast to your Mac) and can't be stored in whole on your Mac or converted to a form that your iPod understands. Such files are often fairly low-fidelity, so even if you could capture them, you'd quickly grow disenchanted with their sound.

If you'd like to try to save some of these streaming files, you can do so with the help of OS X and Wai (Simon) Liu's StreamRipper (http://streamripperx.sourceforge.net). This free tool allows your Mac to capture an audio stream and save it as a file that you can convert to MP3 format. It works only with MP3 streams, however, so don't bother trying to capture RealPlayer files. And, of course, if the source material isn't licensed for capture, using this program to save songs to your Mac and iPod may be a violation of the law.

Play Tunes over a Network

iTunes' tunes needn't be on your Mac's hard drive for you to listen to them. You can stream songs easily from one Mac to the other. Here's how:

1. Mount a network volume that contains music files that you want to stream to your Mac.

2. If you're using iTunes 3, launch iTunes, and choose Preferences from the iTunes menu.

3. In iTunes 3, click the Advanced button in the Preferences dialog box, and uncheck the Copy Files to iTunes Music Folder When Adding to Library check box.

   This option doesn't exist in iTunes 2; iTunes 2 won't copy files to the music folder.

4. In either iTunes 2 or iTunes 3, select the Add to Library command from iTunes' File menu.

5. In the resulting Add to Library dialog box (called Choose Object in iTunes 2), navigate to the mounted volume and then to a folder full of music files.

   This folder may be the iTunes Music folder on another Mac, for example.

6. With the folder highlighted, click Choose.

   Pointers to the music files within that folder will be added to your iTunes library. To play a song on the remote Mac, simply highlight its name and click iTunes' Play button.

Note: If you try to play a tune from a Mac that isn't mounted, iTunes will prompt you to mount the volume.

You can play these files just as you'd play any other song in iTunes. The difference is that they're playing from a remote hard drive, rather than your Mac.

Better yet, because these files are in the Library, the iPod will add them the next time you update the iPod—one somewhat sneaky way to add tunes that aren't located on the Mac that's "sanctioned" to work with the iPod.

In an upcoming version of iTunes, this whole process will be even easier, because iTunes will be able to automatically "discover" and play the iTunes library on another networked Mac, thanks to a Mac OS X networking technology called *Rendezvous*. Although the Rendezvous technology exists, this automatic iTunes discovery feature hasn't been implemented (even though Apple's Steve Jobs demonstrated it at Macworld Expo in July 2002).

Moving music into iTunes

After you've downloaded—and, if necessary, converted—the files you want, you have three ways to move them into iTunes:

- Choose Add to Library from iTunes' File menu.

    When you choose this command, the Add to Library dialog box appears (called Choose Object in iTunes 2). Navigate to the file, folder, or volume you want to add to iTunes, and click Choose (**Figure 2.7**). iTunes will decide which files it thinks it can play and add them to the Library.

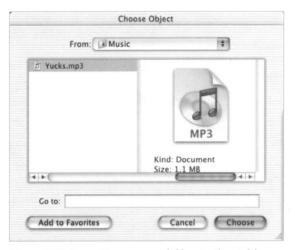

Figure 2.7 Importing a sound file via the Add to Library command.

- Drag files, folders, or entire volumes to the iTunes icon in Mac OS X's Dock, Mac OS 9's tear-off Applications menu, or the iTunes icon in either operating system (at which point iTunes launches and adds the dragged files to the Library).

- Drag files, folders, or entire volumes into iTunes' main window.

    *By default, iTunes 2 keeps its songs in the iTunes Music folder within the iTunes folder inside the Documents folder. (In Mac OS 9, the Documents folder is at the root level of your startup drive; in Mac OS X, the Documents folder is inside your user folder.) When you add tunes to the Library via any of these methods, a dialog box will appear, warning you that should you move these files from their current location; iTunes won't be able to locate them later (**Figure 2.8**).*

Figure 2.8 Although you can keep audio files anywhere you like, iTunes won't be able to locate them if you move them.

iTunes 3 keeps its songs in the iTunes Music folder within the iTunes folder inside the Music folder inside your OS X user folder. So, for example, the path to my iTunes music files would be chris/Music/iTunes/iTunes Music.

Creating and Configuring a Playlist

If the iPod were like lesser MP3 players, all the songs on the device would be selectable from one enormously long list. Thank heavens that Apple's engineers had more sense than to provide you such a limited interface. Among other options, you can navigate your iPod via the playlists you create in iTunes. Here's how to create a variety of playlists.

Standard playlists

You can create standard playlists in both iTunes 2 and iTunes 3. Follow these steps:

1. Click the large plus-sign (+) button in the bottom-left corner of the iTunes window (**Figure 2.9**), or choose the New Playlist command from the File menu (Command-N).

2. Enter a name for your new playlist in the highlighted field that appears next to the new playlist in the Source list (**Figure 2.10**).

Figure 2.9 Click the plus-sign (+) button to create a new playlist.

Figure 2.10
Naming a new playlist.

3. Click the Library entry in the Source list, and select the titles you want to place in the playlist you created.

You can select multiple titles in a row by holding down the Shift key and clicking the first and last titles you want to include. All titles, including the ones you clicked, will be selected via this technique. To select individual titles, hold down the Command key and click the songs you want.

4. Drag the selected titles to the new playlist's icon.

5. Click the new playlist's icon.

The titles you selected have been copied to the new playlist.

6. After you've dragged the titles you want into your playlist, arrange their order.

To do so, click the Number column in the main window, and drag titles up and down in the list. If you attempt to drag titles when any other column heading is selected (Song or Time, for example), the title will plop right back where it came from when you let go of the mouse button. When the iPod is synched with iTunes, this is the order in which the songs will appear in the playlist on your iPod.

You may have noticed that I used the word titles *in the preceding instructions, rather than* songs. *I did this to hint that you're not copying songs from one location on your hard drive to another. You're simply copying the song titles from the Library (the list of all the songs on your hard drive) to another list to make navigation easier. You can play the songs that appear in this playlist by selecting them in the Library as well.*

Playlist from selection

iTunes 2 and iTunes 3 also allow you to create a new playlist from selected items. Here's how to create such a playlist:

1. Select the songs you'd like to appear in the new playlist.

   To select multiple items in a row, click the first item you want in the playlist and then Shift-click the last item. All the songs between (and including) the songs you clicked will be selected.

2. Choose New Playlist from Selection from iTunes' File menu.

   A new untitled playlist appears in the iTunes Source list, containing all the selected songs.

3. To name the playlist, type the name in the highlighted field.

Smart playlists

iTunes 3 introduces the *smart playlist*—a playlist based on user-generated criteria. Smart playlists are not available in iTunes 2. Here's how they work:

1. Choose New Smart Playlist from iTunes' File menu.

   In the resulting Smart Playlist dialog box, you'll see two tabs: Simple and Advanced. To create a simple smart playlist, make sure that you're in the Simple section of the Smart Playlist dialog box.

2. Choose your criteria.

   You'll spy a pop-up menu that allows you to select songs by artist, composer, or genre, followed by a Contains field. To choose all songs by Elvis Presley and Elvis Costello, for example, you'd choose Artist from the pop-up menu and then enter **Elvis** in the Contains field.

   You can limit the selections that appear in the playlist by minutes, hours, megabytes, gigabytes, or number of songs. You may want the playlist to contain no more than 1 GB worth of songs, for example.

   You'll also see a Live Updating option. When switched on, this option will ensure that if you add any songs to iTunes that meet the criteria you've set, those songs will be added to the playlist. If you add a new Elvis Costello album to iTunes, for example, iTunes will update your Elvis smart playlist automatically.

3. Click OK.

A new playlist that contains your smart selections appears in iTunes' Source list.

To create an advanced smart playlist, choose New Smart Playlist from iTunes' File menu and click the Advanced tab in the resulting Smart Playlist dialog box.

The advanced smart playlist allows you to choose songs in many ways (**Figure 2.11**). You can, for example, select songs by album, artist, bit rate, comment, date added, last played, genre, or play count. Clicking the plus-sign (+) button next to a criterion field allows you to add other conditions. You could create a playlist that contains only songs that you've never listened to by punk artists whose names contain the letter J.

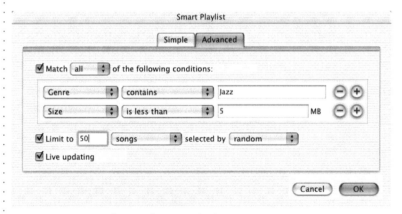

Figure 2.11 An Advanced smart playlist.

As you can with the simple smart playlist, you can limit what appears in the resulting playlist by minutes, hours, megabytes, gigabytes, or number of songs. Advanced smart playlists will also be updated automatically if you choose the Live Updating option.

iTunes 3 includes three smart playlists: My Top Rated, Recently Played, and Top 25 Most Played. As their names imply, My

Top Rated includes 25 songs selected at random that have a rating of four or five stars, Recently Played includes 25 songs selected at random that you've played in the past two weeks, and Top 25 Most Played includes the 25 songs you've played the most often. These playlists have the Live Updating option enabled, which makes it possible for these playlists to be updated dynamically as conditions change (you rate more songs, play different tunes, or play other tunes more often, for example).

Playlist Helpers

Among iTunes 3's other new features are *ratings*, the ability to pass judgment on a song by assigning it a rating of one to five stars; *play count*, a feature that keeps track of the number of times you've played a song in iTunes and on your iPod; and *recently played*, a feature that keeps track of when you last played a song. Here's a quick look at how these features enhance your iPoding experience:

Ratings. Although employing ratings is a fine way to vent your critical spleen (*"I don't care how hefty a royalty it brought the composer, 'Me and You and a Dog Named Boo' was a dreadful waste of vinyl!"*), it's also quite useful. After you rate your songs, you can use those ratings as a playlist criterion.

You can, for example, create a smart playlist that contains nothing but songs with a rating of four stars or more, thus guaranteeing that you hear nothing but your personal favorites. Or, if an ill-favored cousin has planted himself on the living-room sofa for one night too many, create a playlist made up of nothing but one-star wonders, and blast it from one end of the house to the other in a repeating loop.

You can't assign ratings directly to your iPod. Rather, you issue ratings in iTunes 3. You do this by clicking the My Rating column in the main iTunes window and then dragging the pointer to the right. Doing so causes stars to appear in the column. Or, if you prefer doing things as inefficiently as possible, you can click a song title, press Command-I to produce the Song Information window, click the Advanced tab, and drag your pointer in the My Ratings field to produce the desired number of stars. (Okay, one instance in which assigning ratings this way isn't inefficient is when you want to assign the same rating to a batch of songs. Just select all the songs to which you want to assign a rating; press Command-I; and, in the resulting Multiple Song Information window, check the box next to the My Rating field. Now issue a rating in that same field. The rating you create will be assigned to all selected songs.)

continues on next page

Playlist Helpers *continued*

Play count. The ability to keep track of the number of times you've played a song is also helpful when you want to create a playlist. One might reasonably assume that if you've played some songs more than others, those tunes hold a special place in your heart. By using play count as a smart-playlist criterion, you could take all songs that you've played more than 10 times, shove them into a playlist, and— using the batch-rating technique I mention earlier in this sidebar— rate all the songs in that playlist with five stars.

Or you could use play count as a way to limit songs you've played to death. In this case, create a smart playlist of songs that you've never heard. Play this group of tunes when you'd like to listen to some fresh material.

iTunes 3 keeps track of play count in the Play Count column of the main iTunes window. The iPod tracks play count in the Top 25 Most Played playlist in the iPod's Playlists screen.

Recently played. The name says it all. Both iTunes 3 and the iPod keep track of when you last played a song. This information is reflected in iTunes 3 in the Last Played column of iTunes' main window. On the iPod, songs most recently played appear in the Recently Played playlist in the iPod's Playlists screen.

You can also use the recently played criterion to create a smart playlist comprised of fresh material (or tunes you just can't get enough of).

Both iTunes 3 and the iPod keep track of play counts and recently played status. This status won't change on the iPod, however, until you connect the iPod to your Mac and update it. You can play Nick Lowe's "Truth Drug" 17 times in a row on your iPod, for example, but it won't appear in the Recently Played or Top 25 Most Played playlists until you update your iPod in iTunes 3. (Note that the Live Updating option must be switched on in these playlists for this feature to work.) When you update the iPod, the play-count tally is increased in iTunes 3 to reflect the number of times you played particular tunes on your iPod.

Moving Music to the iPod

The conduit for moving music to the iPod is iTunes—which, fortunately, is fairly flexible about how it goes about the process. The key to determining how you move your tunes is the iPod Preferences dialog box.

To produce the dialog box, plug your iPod into your Mac's FireWire port, and launch iTunes. (By default, iTunes will launch on its own when you connect the iPod.) Click the iPod's icon in the iTunes Source list (**Figure 2.12**).

Figure 2.12
My iPod in the
Source list.

When you do, you'll see that a new icon appears next to the EQ icon in the bottom-right corner of the iTunes window (**Figure 2.13**). Click this iPod icon to open the iPod Preferences dialog box (**Figure 2.14**).

Figure 2.13 The iPod Preferences icon appears at the bottom of the iTunes window when you select the iPod in the Source list.

Figure 2.14
The iPod
Preferences
dialog box.

In the following sections, I'll give you a close look at this dialog box's various options.

Automatically Update All Songs and Playlists

When you choose this option, iTunes will take a gander at what's on the iPod, and add songs in its Library and remove songs on the iPod that are not in its Library.

Although everyone will be pleased that iTunes automatically adds songs from the iTunes Library, not everyone may be tickled by the notion that it also erases songs. If you've removed songs from iTunes' Library and want them to remain on your iPod after the update, this option is not for you.

This option is on by default.

Automatically Update Selected Playlists Only

This option updates only the playlists you've selected. Any songs stored on your iPod that don't belong to the selected playlists will be erased when you select this option.

This option is a good one to use when several members of your family are sharing an iPod. Mom can pack a playlist with hits from the '60s, and when it's her day with the iPod, she can update only her playlist and—to make room for her tunes—erase Little Johnny's Speed Metal selections. When Dad can wrestle the iPod away from Mom, he can lose the '60s and update the iPod with his be-bop collection.

Again, this option isn't a good idea when you don't want items to be removed from your iPod.

Manually Manage Songs and Playlists

Ah, finally—the option to use when you want to add songs to your iPod without removing any tunes from the device. When you select this option, all the playlists on your iPod will appear below the iPod's icon in iTunes' Source list. To add songs to the iPod, just select them in the Library or one of iTunes' playlists, and drag them to one of the iPod's playlists (**Figure 2.15**). The songs will appear at the top of the playlist. To move a song's position, click the top of the Number column, and drag the song to where you'd like it to appear in the list.

Figure 2.15 Moving a song to the iPod manually.

If you don't care to add songs to an existing playlist on your iPod, feel free to create a new playlist. Just click the icon of your iPod in the Source list and then click the New Playlist button (the + button) at the bottom of the Source list to add an empty playlist to the iPod. Name the playlist by typing its name in the highlighted field.

To remove songs from the iPod, select the songs you want to remove; then either press the Mac's Delete key or drag the songs to the Trash on the Desktop (or, in the case of OS X, to the Trash in the Dock). You'll be asked to confirm that you really want to delete the songs. (You can disable this warning by clicking the Don't Ask Me Again check box in the warning dialog box.)

You can even copy entire playlists to other playlists by dragging one playlist icon on top of another. This method works for both iTunes and iPod playlists.

When you remove songs from your iPod, you don't remove them from your Mac. Unless you select a song in iTunes' Library and delete it, the song is still on your Mac's hard drive.

When you choose to manage your songs and playlists manually, you'll be told that you have to disconnect the iPod manually—meaning that you have to take action to unmount the thing rather than simply unplug it from your Mac. To do so, you can select the iPod in the Source list and then click the Eject button in the bottom-right corner of the iTunes window, or move to the Finder and drag the iPod to the Trash. When its icon disappears from the Desktop, you can unplug your iPod. The iPod will also tell you when it's ready to be unmounted. When the iPod is mounted on your computer or busy accepting data from an application, the display flashes the international symbol for "Back off, Jack!" (the circle with a line through it), along with a "Do not disconnect" message. When you unmount it properly, the iPod displays a large checkmark and the message "OK to disconnect."

One more unexpected pleasure offered by the manual-update option is the ability to play songs on your iPod through the attached Mac's speakers. With manual update switched on, just select a song in your iPod and press the Mac's spacebar. The song will stream off the iPod, through iTunes, and out your Mac's speakers or headphone port. To control the volume, you must use iTunes' volume control; the iPod's controls won't work in this mode.

Copy Restrictions

The iPod was designed as a one-way copying device. You can move music from your Mac to your iPod, but you can't move music from the iPod to the Mac. Apple designed the iPod this way to discourage music piracy. The company might very well have run into some legal problems were the iPod shown to be a portable conduit for moving music from one computer to another.

For this same reason, the iPod is tied to one Macintosh. When you plug your iPod into a Mac other than the one it was originally plugged into, and that iPod is configured to be updated automatically, a warning dialog box appears, indicating that the iPod is linked to another iTunes Library (**Figure 2.16**). You'll be given the option to leave the iPod as is or have its contents replaced by the current Mac's iTunes Library. If you choose to leave the iPod as is, you can't add songs to its Library until you open the iPod Preferences dialog box and choose the "manually manage" option. After you do, you can copy songs freely from that Mac's iTunes Library to the iPod.

But that leaves you in a bit of a quandary, for when you return your iPod to the original Mac, if you turn on one of the automatic-update options, the songs you copied from the other Mac will be erased from the iPod, because they don't exist in the iTunes Library of the original Mac. You could simply manage your iPod manually from that day forward, of course, but that pretty well ruptures the convenient relationship between iTunes and the iPod.

Alternatives to this manual-mode scheme? You could copy the song you want from the original CD to both Macs (provided that you own the CD, of course). Or you could burn a CD of MP3 files that exist on one Mac and copy those files to the other Mac (again, provided that you own the original material). If you *don't* own the original material—and no, downloading it from the Internet or borrowing your friend's copy of the CD doesn't count—do your conscience a favor and buy the CD.

The iPod "Chris Breen's iPod" is linked to another iTunes music library. Do you want to change the link to this iTunes music library and replace all existing songs and playlists on this iPod with those from this library?

No   Yes

Figure 2.16
The iPod was designed to synchronize with one Mac at a time.

Open iTunes When Attached

On by default, this option fires up iTunes when you plug your iPod into your Mac's FireWire port. This option is reasonably convenient unless you're using your iPod strictly as an external FireWire drive. Because I do use my iPod for exactly this purpose, I keep this option switched off.

Enable FireWire Disk Use

Speaking of using your iPod as an external FireWire drive, this option makes it happen. When this option is switched on, your iPod appears on the Desktop and can be used just like any other hard drive. To copy files to the iPod, just drag them to the iPod icon. Likewise, you can move files from the iPod by double-clicking the iPod to open it and then dragging the files you want from the iPod to your Mac.

> *You can't use this method to move your music files from the*
> *iPod to the Mac, however, and the music files you drag to*
> *the iPod's icon won't appear in iTunes. I'll discuss this issue*
> *at length in Chapter 4. Suffice it to say for now that the music*
> *files you play on your iPod are hidden away so that you won't*
> *be tempted to copy them to a multitude of computers.*

When you choose the "manually manage" option, your iPod is configured as an external drive automatically, and this option is selected but grayed out. If you select one of the automatic options, you must enable this option for the iPod to appear on the Desktop.

When you use the iPod as an external hard drive, you must unmount it manually. You can do this by employing one of the usual Finder techniques for unmounting a volume (dragging the iPod icon to the Trash, Control-clicking the icon and choosing Eject from the contextual menu, or choosing Eject from the File menu in OS X) or by clicking the iPod icon in iTunes' Source list and then clicking iTunes' Eject button.

Only Update Checked Songs

As its name hints, this option tells iTunes to update those songs that are checked in iTunes' Library. This option can act as a safety measure so that songs that may no longer be available to iTunes (the songs you pulled from a networked volume by following the advice in the "Play Tunes over a Network" sidebar earlier in the chapter, for example) aren't erased from your iPod during an automatic update.

The Get Info Window

If you peek in iTunes' File menu, you'll find the Get Info command. Choosing this command (or pressing Command-I) produces the Song Information dialog box (**Figure 2.17**) for the selected song (or songs). You needn't be concerned about a lot of what goes on in this dialog box; some settings apply only to iTunes. But it is worth your while to look at the portion of the dialog box that appears when you click the Tags tab.

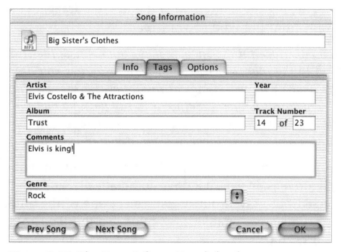

Figure 2.17 The Song Information dialog box.

In the Tags tab, you'll find Artist and Album fields (along with the Title field, which appears at the top of every tab in this dialog box). The information in these fields is carried over to the iPod. You may find occasions when it's helpful to change the information in these fields. If you have two versions of the same song—one from the CD and another as a live recording—you could change the song title of the latter to include "(Live)." Or if you discover that the iPod splits an artist into different groupings—Elvis Costello and Elvis Costello and the Attractions, for example—and you'd like all the songs by that artist to appear below a single heading, you can edit the Artist field.

Although you could click the Next and Previous buttons to change the settings of adjacent songs in the Library, it's not always necessary. To change these fields in a group of songs, select a bunch of tunes in the Library, Shift-click the first and last songs in the series of titles you want to edit, or Command-click to select individual songs and then press Command-I. This action produces the Multiple Song Information dialog box (**Figure 2.18**), where you can change the Artist, Title, and Comments fields for every selected song in one fell swoop.

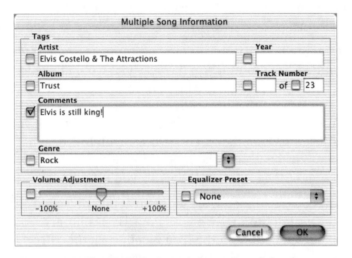

Figure 2.18 The Multiple Song Information dialog box.

You may recall from Chapter 1 that the equalizer settings you impose in iTunes carry over to the iPod. You can also change the equalizer preset for all the songs you've selected by choosing a preset from the Equalizer Preset pop-up menu. If you want to change the EQ settings for a single song, select that song, press Command-I, click the Options tab in the resulting Song Information dialog box, and choose a preset from the Equalizer Preset pop-up menu.

Sound Check

Sound Check is a feature added with the October 2002 iPods and iTunes 3. (Sorry, it's not available in iTunes 2.) This feature attempts to address an all-too-common problem: the volume among songs (particularly songs from different albums) varies to the point where you must fiddle with the iPod's volume control constantly to maintain a consistent sound level.

When Sound Check is engaged, it analyzes the volume levels of all the songs in iTunes' library, and boosts the volume of quieter tunes so that their level more closely matches that of louder songs. This doesn't mean that Sound Check will alter individual volumes within a single tune—in other words, the *pianissimo* passages in the Rubenstein recording of Chopin's *Nocturnes* won't suddenly become *fortissimo*. Rather, the overall volume of those *Nocturnes* will be raised, so you won't feel compelled to crank the volume after listening to Mahler's *8th Symphony*.

In designing this feature, Apple had to make some trade-offs. For Sound Check to function flawlessly, it would have to spend hours analyzing your iTunes library. Knowing that its customers were unlikely to put up with such seemingly endless analysis, Apple designed Sound Check so that it brings volumes closer together than they were before—with the idea that while you may not be able to completely give up fiddling with the volume in iTunes' and on the iPod, you'd fiddle less often.

To make Sound Check work on your iPod, you must first tell Sound Check to do its stuff with your iTunes library. To do so, choose Preferences from the iPod menu, click the Effects button to open the Effects dialog box, and click the Sound Check option (**Figure 2.19**). When you click OK in the Preferences dialog box, iTunes will begin analyzing the songs in iTunes' library.

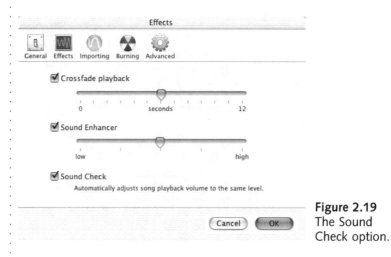

Figure 2.19
The Sound Check option.

When your iPod is next updated, its music files will be ready for the Sound Check feature. To switch it on, choose Settings in the iPod's main screen, select Sound Check, and press the Select button to choose On.

Audible.com

Audible.com is a company that sells downloadable spoken-word content: books, magazine articles, and news, for example. iTunes 3 can play this material, as well as burn it to CD-R and transfer it to the iPod.

Downloading and playing spoken-word files

iTunes 3 and the iPod Software 1.2 Updater bring Audible.com compatibility to iTunes and the iPod for Macintosh. (Audible.com support isn't available with the software bundled with the Windows version of the iPod.) The feature works this way.

1. Launch iTunes 3, choose Preferences from the iTunes menu, click the General button in the resulting window, and click the Set button next to Use iTunes for Internet Music Playback.

2. Log onto the Web, and point your browser to *www.audible.com*.

3. When you're on the site, find something that you'd like to download (a novel, for example), and click the Add to Basket button.

4. Click the Checkout button on the page that appears.

5. If you don't have an Audible.com account, you'll be asked to set one up.

   Doing so requires that you submit your name and email address and that you create a user name and password. When you make a purchase, you'll be asked for a credit-card number and more extensive contact information (street address and phone number).

6. Review the charges on the next page, and click the Proceed With Purchase button.

   The purchase will be processed. After the file is processed, you'll be taken to a page that lists the order number of your purchase and provides links to My Library, a storage area for any Audible.com files you've purchased.

7. Click the My Library link.

   You should see your file (or files, if you've purchased more than one).

8. Click the Get it Now button next to the file you want to download.

9. In the window that appears, select a format for the file you want to download.

   The Mac and iPod support formats 2, 3, and 4. Format 2 files are the smallest and the lowest resolution (meaning that they don't sound very good). Format 3 files are larger (and sound better) than Format 2 files. Format 4 files are the largest of all and, as you might expect, are of the highest quality.

10. Select a format, and click the Download button.

    Don't worry—you haven't committed to downloading the file in this one format alone. You're welcome to return to My Library and download the file again in another format (or this same format, if you like).

11. Double-click the downloaded file.

    It should open in iTunes 3. (If it doesn't, launch iTunes 3, and drag the file into iTunes' main window.)

12. If this is the first time you've used an Audible.com file, enter your Audible.com user name and password when iTunes asks you to do so.

    After you enter that information, iTunes will log onto the Web and register your Mac with Audible.com.

When you next update your iPod, any Audible.com files that you've downloaded will be moved to your iPod.

Registering Your Computers

Audible.com requires you to register your computer with the service to keep you from sharing Audible.com files with other users. You are allowed to register three computers per Audible.com account; each will be registered under your Audible.com user name. Audible.com files won't play on unregistered computers, so if you've already registered three computers, you won't be able to play an Audible.com file on a fourth computer.

To work around this problem, you must unregister one of your computers. (You'll find the appropriate option in iTunes 3's Advanced menu.) Then you can register a different computer. Audible.com files won't play on computers that have been unregistered until you reregister the computer.

Although the iPod doesn't count against Audible.com's three-computer registration limit, you can download Audible.com files to an iPod from only two of those three computers. Should you attempt to download an Audible.com file from a third computer, iTunes won't download the file to your iPod.

Audible.com tips

Apple and Audible.com have done their best to make downloading and playing these files as easy as possible, but there are a few tricks you should know:

- You needn't worry about losing your place when playing an Audible.com file. When you stop playing the file in either iTunes 3 or on your iPod, the file will be bookmarked so that when you play the file next, it begins playing from the spot where you left off.

  Better yet, if you listen to the file in both iTunes 3 and on your iPod—a chapter of a novel on your iPod while you're driving to work and a chapter on your office Mac when you're supposed to be preparing the company's quarterly earnings statement, for example—the bookmark will be synchronized between the iPod and Mac the next time you update your iPod. If, for instance, you most recently played the file on your Mac, iTunes will update the bookmark on your iPod so that it matches the bookmark in iTunes.

- If your Mac relies on a proxy server to access the Internet, iTunes won't be able to register your computer with

Audible.com; therefore, you won't be able to play Audible.com files. If you're in such a situation, find another way to get to the Web—via a dial-up connection, for example. You need to make this alternative connection just once—long enough for the computer to be registered with Audible.com.

- The following tip doesn't apply directly to the iPod, but it's a confusing-enough aspect of Audible.com that it's worth mentioning.

If you've attempted to burn an Audio.com file that exceeds 74 minutes in iTunes 3, you've undoubtedly been frustrated by the warning that the operation cannot proceed because the file you want to burn exceeds the recordable length of a CD. So how do you transfer your Audible.com books to CD? Just so:

1. Create a new playlist in iTunes, and drag your Audible.com file from the Library to this playlist.

2. Open the playlist, and click the file's title.

3. Now press Command-I to produce the Song Information window.

4. Click the Options tab, and enter **1:14:00** in the Stop Time field.

   This entry tells Disc Burner to burn only the first 74 minutes of audio—the amount of audio that you can safely burn to a CD-R—to the disc.

5. Click OK.

6. Click the Burn CD icon.

7. When you're instructed to do so, insert a blank CD-R.

8. Once again, click Burn CD to record the audio to disc.

To record the next 74 minutes of audio, follow this same procedure, but this time, enter **1:14:00** in the Start Time field and **2:28:00** in the Stop Time field. Repeat for each succeeding 74 minutes of audio.

Other iTunes Tricks

What other changes can you make in iTunes that will make a difference to your iPod?

- **Change the iPod's name.** When your iPod appears on the Desktop or in iTunes, it has a name—Mr. iPod, for example. If you've decided that your iPod is of the female, rather than male, persuasion, you might want to change its name to Ms. iPod. To do so, click the iPod's name on the Desktop, wait for the name to highlight, and enter its new name. Or click the iPod entry in the iTunes Source list to highlight the device, click the name to highlight it, and enter a new name.

  This new name will appear in the iPod's Info window when the iPod is next updated.

- **Separately change the view settings for the iPod.** In iTunes' Edit menu, you'll find the View Options command. You use this command to determine the kind of information iTunes displays about items in the main window—the year songs were recorded and the date they were added to the Library, for example. Although you may want to sort tunes in the Library six ways to Sunday, you may be less inclined to do so when you view the information on your iPod (particularly because the iPod can't display a lot of these categories). Fortunately, you don't have to. You can create different view settings for every item in the Source List—including the iPod and each playlist on it.

- **View iTunes Visuals.** Yes, when you play songs from the iPod through your Mac (see the section where I discuss managing your iPod manually), you can switch on iTunes Visuals (Command-T)—the program's groovy light-show feature. Visuals respond to the iPod's music just as they would to a song played directly on your Mac, though you may find that they react a bit more slowly when you play from the iPod.

- **iTunes AppleScripts.** Apple offers a host of helpful AppleScripts for iTunes that allow you to do such things as look up the entire output of an artist on the Web.

Included in these AppleScripts is the iPod Library Summary script, which you'll find in the AppleScript menu when you add these scripts (**Figure 2.20**). When you highlight your iPod's name in the Source list and sort your iPod's tunes by Artist, this script generates a text file that includes the artist, album, song title, and play time of every song on your iPod. This file is tab-delimited and can be imported easily into a spreadsheet application such as AppleWorks or Microsoft Excel.

The AppleScripts aren't included by default. To download them, go to *www.apple.com/applescript/itunes*. This page provides not only download links to the scripts, but also instructions for installing them.

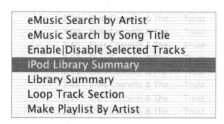

Figure 2.20
A helpful AppleScript can be yours for the downloading.

- **iPod help.** If you have an iPod, you know that the manual is pretty insubstantial. When you want to get help with your iPod (I mean, other than in the pages of this quite-helpful book), choose iPod Help from iTunes' Help menu (**Figure 2.21**).

Figure 2.21
Need help? You'll find it here.

Of iPods and PCs

No, your eyes don't deceive you. Although the iPod is an Apple product from cover to core, Microsoft Windows users are just as welcome to slide into the iPod groove as their Mac-using companions.

This hasn't always been the case. When the iPod was first released, it was intended to be compatible with Macs only (though a couple of third-party utilities allowed you to use a Mac iPod with Windows—I'll show you how later in this chapter). But it didn't take Apple long to realize that a fair number of Windows users were also enthusiastic about owning an iPod.

Apple hoped that these Windows folk would be so enthralled with this diminutive device that they'd purchase a Mac simply so they could use it with an iPod. And some did.

Once Apple determined that it had sold about as many iPod/Macintosh combo platters as it was likely to, it set about creating an iPod for Windows. This model would vary little from the Mac iPod. It would require a hard drive formatted to be compatible with the Windows operating system, Windows-compatible software for downloading music to the device, and a FireWire adapter for use with FireWire cards that bore the smaller 4-pin FireWire connector found on some PCs.

This is the Windows iPod that Apple announced in July 2002 and shipped the following September.

In this chapter we'll look at that iPod, how to make the best use of it in Windows, and how you can make your iPod—whether designed for Mac or PC—the most comfortable with either computing platform.

Configuring Your PC

You're a PC user with a purpose. You just purchased an iPod and a copy of this book, and you're ready to make the most of Windows and your iPod. You attach the iPod's FireWire cable to the appropriate receptacle on the top of the iPod, grab the other end of the cable, and climb behind your PC in what turns out to be a completely vain search for a compatible port. You see, chances are that if you hunt around on the back of most PCs, a FireWire (also known as an IEEE 1394 or iLink) port is nowhere to be seen.

Whatever name you care to call it, FireWire is a protocol developed by Apple. Microsoft and Intel generally steer clear of Apple protocols because (a) Apple often requires a licensing fee and Microsoft and Intel would rather skirt such fees, and (b) Microsoft and Intel have a natural reluctance to push a technology that it hasn't developed. (Why promote FireWire when Intel offers its own transfer protocol, USB 2.0, for example?) It's probably for these reasons that Microsoft and Intel declined to embrace the FireWire standard—the result being that for several years, PCs did not have FireWire ports.

Sony and several other digital-media companies knew a good thing when they saw it, however, and did equip some of their hardware (camcorders in particular) with FireWire ports. Despite Microsoft's and Intel's lack of interest, FireWire became *the* standard for connecting digital camcorders with computers. If the Big Boys in the PC market wanted a bigger piece of the digital-video pie, they would have to swallow their pride, provide FireWire drivers for Windows, and start placing FireWire ports on PCs.

As I wrote the second edition of this book in the waning weeks of 2002, this change was made only very recently. If you have a PC made before 2002, it likely lacks a FireWire port. But this doesn't mean that you should return your iPod (or, heaven forbid, this book!). Fortunately, adding FireWire to your PC is a simple matter. The following sections show you how.

Making the connection: hardware

The means to get FireWire on your PC is a FireWire host adapter card. If you have a desktop PC, this card will be designed for your PC's PCI slots (**Figure 3.1**). If you have a laptop with a PC Card slot, look for a FireWire PC card. These FireWire cards are made by such companies as Adaptec (*www.adaptec.com*), Belkin (*www.belkin.com*), Keyspan (*www.keyspan.com*), and Orange Micro (*www.orangemicro.com*). PCI FireWire cards cost $35 to $75, and FireWire CardBus cards hover around $100.

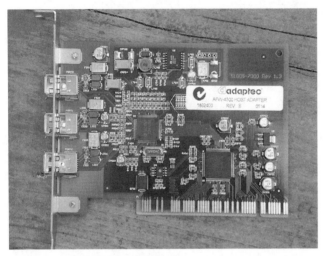

Figure 3.1 A PCI FireWire card.

To add a FireWire card to your PC, that PC must have an available PCI or Card slot and should be equipped with a 266 MHz or faster processor. (350 MHz really is the base limit if you also plan to use this card for digital video.) You must be running Microsoft Windows 98 Second Edition (SE), ME, 2000, or XP (both the Home and Professional editions support FireWire).

If you're running Windows 98 SE, consider upgrading. FireWire made its first appearance in Windows 98 SE, and quite frankly, Microsoft didn't do a terribly good job of implementing it. Transfer rates can be slower than in later revisions of Windows, and these early FireWire drivers don't always see eye to eye with the iPod.

Installing a PCI card

Now that you're sure that your PC is up to snuff, here's how to install the card in a desktop PC:

1. Turn off the PC, and disconnect the cables running into it—video, mouse, keyboard, USB, modem, Ethernet, sound, and power.

2. Open the PC.

   See your PC's manual if you're unsure how to do this.

3. Touch the PC's power supply (that big silver box on the inside) to discharge any static electricity you may be carrying around with you.

   Static electricity can destroy delicate computer components.

4. Remove the FireWire PCI card from its staticproof bag.

5. Locate a free PCI slot (it's probably white with a single notch), and remove the metal cover that blocks access to the slot from the back of the PC (**Figure 3.2**).

6. Insert the card, and screw it into place (**Figure 3.3**).

Figure 3.2 PCI slots are usually white.

Figure 3.3 The FireWire PCI card in place.

7. Reconnect any cables you disconnected.

8. Restart your PC.

Installing a PC card

The PC card slot was designed so that it would be a dead cinch to add devices such as Ethernet, modem, USB, media reader, and FireWire cards to your laptop. It is. To install a FireWire PC card to your PC, simply shove the card into the PC card slot. You should be able to do this with the laptop running, but check the instructions that came with the card, in case the manufacturer wants things done differently.

> *Note that a FireWire PC card may not provide power to your iPod (check the documentation that comes with the card to learn if power is part of the package). This means that you can't charge your iPod from your laptop PC. If your card doesn't provide power, you must charge the iPod prior to plugging it into your laptop or use an adapter such as SiK's FireJuice adapter (for more information on this adapter see Chapter 7).*

Completing the connection: software

You may have a little or a lot to do to configure your new FireWire card, depending on the card you get and how Windows likes it. Windows can be the tiniest bit unpredictable and you may have to install some kind of driver software to make your PC work with the FireWire card. Or Windows may be more than happy to do the job for you by installing its own FireWire driver. Please let the manual be your guide.

After you install your card and reboot Windows (or—in the case of a laptop and PC card—insert the card), Windows may see the card and install the appropriate drivers automatically when the PC boots up. If Windows does install the drivers, it may ask you to reboot your PC. Do so.

Thereafter, these are the steps you're likely to take in Windows XP:

1. After Windows has rebooted, right-click My Computer, and choose Properties from the resulting contextual menu (**Figure 3.4**).

Open
Explore
Search...
Manage

Map Network Drive...
Disconnect Network Drive...

Create Shortcut
Delete
Rename

Properties

Figure 3.4
Choose Properties
from My Computer's
contextual menu.

The System Properties dialog box opens.

2. Click the Hardware tab and then the Device Manager button, and look for the appropriate entry for your FireWire card. On my PC it's listed under SBP2 IEEE 1394 Devices.

3. Click the plus sign next to the 1394 entry to reveal the name of the FireWire card you've inserted (**Figure 3.5**).

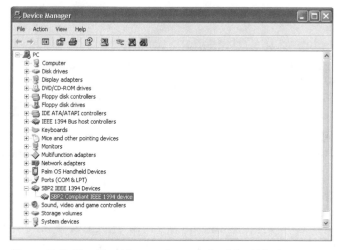

Figure 3.5 The FireWire card recognized by Windows.

4. Select this name and right-click to reveal the contextual menu. Select Properties from this menu.

In the Device Status section of the resulting window, you should see the message "This device is working properly" (**Figure 3.6**).

Figure 3.6
Windows' reassurance
that the FireWire card
actually works.

If you see anything other than this message, check
the manual that came with the card, and pray that it
features a troubleshooting section. If no help is offered
there, check the card manufacturer's Web site for
help. You may have to get an updated driver or
reconfigure Windows.

iPod for Windows software

Included with the iPod for Windows is a CD-ROM that contains the drivers necessary for the iPod to be recognized by
Windows, a Windows version of the iPod Software Updater (a
utility necessary for updating or restoring the iPod's software),
and a copy of MusicMatch's (*www.musicmatch.com*) Music-
Match Jukebox Pro. This latter application lets you play the
music files on your PC and iPod, burn music files to CD-R and
CD-RW discs, and download music to your iPod.

Installing the iPod Software

If you've installed just about any other Windows application,
there are no surprises here. When you insert the iPod for
Windows disc, an installer application opens and you're walked
through the installation process. Although installing the software is anything but challenging, there are a few points worth
mentioning.

iPod Software installation

Early in the installation process the software will ask for your iPod's serial number and tell you that it can be found on the back of the iPod. If you have extraordinarily good vision (or a decent magnifying glass) you may be able to make out the miniscule number printed on the shiny back of the iPod. I can't.

Thankfully, you can find the serial number in two other locations. The first is on the iPod's display screen. Just fire up the iPod, choose the About command in the main iPod screen, and press Select. You'll find the serial number at the bottom of the resulting About screen. You can also find the iPod's serial number on the outside of the box that the iPod came in (not on the outer sleeve but on the gray inner box).

A bit later in the process you'll be presented with a window that asks for registration information—your name, address, phone number, and email address, for example. It's a good idea to register your iPod so that if you ever have problems with it, Apple has a record of ownership. However, you can install the software without registering the iPod. Just click the Next button in the Registration Information to proceed with installation.

MusicMatch Jukebox installation

When the installer finishes placing the components necessary for Windows to work with the iPod on your PC's hard drive, the MusicMatch Jukebox installer launches. This installer would like a little personal information as well.

As with the previous registration screen, you can refrain from providing your name and email address. You must, however, indicate the year you were born. Apparently there are laws on the books that lend a greater degree of privacy to those under the age of 13. If you enter a year-of-birth that places you among this under-13 group, the registration screen won't allow you to enter personal information.

The Personal Music Recommendations window follows. In this window you can choose to allow MusicMatch to collect data on the kind of music you listen to so that it can send you links to downloadable music it thinks you'll like. Just between us,

I consider my musical habits my own and have selected the No option in this window. If you find such a service desirable, click Yes with my blessing.

Once you've made your choice and clicked Next, the installation will proceed—installing the application and plug-in driver necessary for MusicMatch Jukebox to recognize the iPod as a portable music device.

You'll then be asked to enter a user upgrade key. This is the number on the outside of the iPod Software for Windows CD sleeve that enables MusicMatch Jukebox's Pro features—the ability to rip music files and burn CDs more quickly, for example. Enter this number and you're good to go—the installation process completes and MusicMatch Jukebox opens by default.

I pray that this tip will be unnecessary by the time your eyes pass over these words. But as I write this, one of the very first things you see when MusicMatch Jukebox launches for the first time is a pop-up tip that tells you to check MusicMatch's Web site for the latest update to MusicMatch Jukebox. As tempting as this sounds, check with MusicMatch's Web site before you download an update. As I write this, the update offered by MusicMatch is not compatible with the iPod.

MusicMatch Jukebox overview

MusicMatch Jukebox is comprised of a few different windows. The main window contains the play controls to the left and the Playlists area to the right (**Figure 3.7**). You can hide the Playlists area by clicking on the left-pointing triangle on the right side of the window.

Figure 3.7 MusicMatch Jukebox's Main window with Play controls and Playlists area.

The My Library window contains a column view of all the songs in your music library (**Figure 3.8**). You can change the view in which your library is displayed—view by artist, album, or genre, for example. Songs are clumped together in folders, depending on the view you've selected. For example, if you've chosen to view by artist, all John Cale songs are placed in a single folder. View this same library by album and you'll see John Cale's *Paris 1919, Helen of Troy,* and *Slow Dazzle* albums broken out into separate folders.

Figure 3.8 The MusicMatch Jukebox Library window.

When you plug in your iPod and launch MusicMatch Jukebox, the Portable Devices window appears (**Figure 3.9**). It's in this window that you view the songs on your iPod, manually synchronize your music library and iPod, and gain access to the iPod's options via the Option button (including the ability to edit the iPod's name and determine whether it's automatically updated when you plug it into your PC). I'll discuss each of these windows and functions at greater length in this chapter.

Figure 3.9 MusicMatch Jukebox's Portable Devices window.

Ripping a CD

Your iPod wouldn't be much of a music player if it had no music on it. The first thing you'll want to do is move some music from the most likely source—an audio CD—into MusicMatch Jukebox. Here's how to go about it:

1. Launch MusicMatch Jukebox.

2. Insert an audio CD into an available CD drive.

   Older versions of Windows may open and play the CD with MusicMatch Jukebox. If you're running Windows XP (Home or Professional), a window will appear that asks what you'd like to do with the CD—play it with Windows Media Player, play it with MusicMatch Jukebox, view the files it contains with Windows Explorer, or take no action. For now, select the option to play the audio CD in MusicMatch Jukebox.

   If your PC has an always-on connection to the Internet (if you have a cable or DSL connection, for example), MusicMatch Jukebox will venture out onto the Web and download such track information as title, artist, and length of each song on the CD.

   If you have a penchant for tedious tasks (or no information is available online for the CD you've inserted), you're welcome to manually enter song information.

3. To convert (or *rip*) the audio files on the CD to your hard drive, click the red Record button in Music-Match Jukebox's main window (**Figure 3.10**).

   When you do, the Recorder window appears. In this window you can select which of the tracks on the disc you'd like to rip (by default all tracks are selected).

Record button

Figure 3.10
Press the Record button to rip an audio CD.

4. Press Record in the Recorder window and MusicMatch Jukebox begins ripping the CD—showing the progress its making as a percentage of each song ripped.

When MusicMatch Jukebox finishes ripping the CD, a fanfare erupts from your PC's speakers and the disc is automatically ejected.

Moving Music into MusicMatch Jukebox

Ripping a CD isn't the only way to get music in MusicMatch Jukebox. You may, for example, download music from the Web or you may have moved some music you own from another computer onto your PC via a network connection. This music can be added to MusicMatch Jukebox as well.

- Choose Add New Music Track(s) to Library from MusicMatch Jukebox's File menu.

When you select this command, the Add Tracks to Library dialog box appears. From within this dialog box you can navigate to specific folders that contain music. Or, you can take the shotgun approach and select a volume (your C drive, for example) and click the Add button (**Figure 3.11**). MusicMatch Jukebox will scan that volume for any compatible music files it can find and add them to the library.

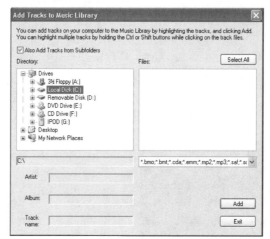

Figure 3.11
Adding tracks to your music library.

Choosing the shotgun method is likely to turn up such interesting musical tidbits as the Microsoft toe-tapper "Windows Welcome music" (all 5 minutes and 24 seconds of it!).

- Drag a compatible music file into the MusicMatch Jukebox's Playlist or Library window.

  Dragging the file into the Playlist window causes the song to begin playing immediately, but doesn't add it to MusicMatch Jukebox's library. To add it to a playlist, click the Save button just below the Playlist window. To add the file to your library, drag the file into the Library window.

  By default, MusicMatch Jukebox keeps its songs in the My Music folder within the My Documents folder (within your user folder if you're running Windows XP). You can instruct MusicMatch Jukebox to use an additional folder for music storage by selecting Settings from the Options menu, clicking the Music Library tab, and in the Library Auto-Load section of the window, clicking the Browse button to select a folder to "watch." When new music files are added to this watched folder, they will appear in MusicMatch Jukebox's library.

Creating and Configuring a Playlist

As with iTunes and the Macintosh iPod, MusicMatch Jukebox allows you to organize your library of songs in playlists. To create such a playlist, follow these steps:

1. Launch MusicMatch Jukebox. If the Library window doesn't appear, click the My Library button at the lower-left of the MusicMatch window.

2. Select the songs you'd like to add to your playlist. Right-click one of the selected songs and select Add Track(s) to Playlist from the contextual menu (**Figure 3.12**). Alternatively, select Music Library from MusicMatch Jukebox's Options menu and then Add Track(s) to Playlist from the submenu.

Figure 3.12
Select some tunes and
invoke this command to
add tracks to a playlist.

3. Once the songs have appeared in the Playlists window, arrange the order in which you'd like the songs to play (**Figure 3.13**). To do so, simply drag songs up or down in the list.

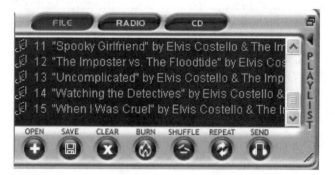

Figure 3.13 Your songs appear in the Playlists area.

When you have the playlist configured to your satisfaction, click the Save button that appears just below the Playlist window.

4. A Save Playlist dialog box appears where you enter a name for your new playlist. Once you've named it, press Save.

5. To clear the songs from the playlist, press the Clear button below the Playlists window.

   This doesn't remove the songs from your library, it simply clears the playlist so you can create or call up other playlists.

6. To call up a playlist, press the Open button below the Playlists window, click the Playlists button in the resulting Open Music dialog box, and click the Play button.

The playlist will load in the Playlists window and the first song in the playlist will begin playing.

Moving Music to the iPod

MusicMatch Jukebox offers you a couple of ways to transfer music from your PC to the iPod. As with iTunes and the iPod you can cause the iPod to be updated each time you plug it into your PC. Or, you could manually update it. The key to managing music on your iPod is the Options dialog box, available from the MusicMatch Jukebox's Portable Devices window. Let's take a look.

The Portable Devices window

By default, when you plug your iPod into your PC, MusicMatch Jukebox opens along with the Portable Devices window. The iPod appears under the Attached Portable Devices entry in the left pane of this window.

If you click on the iPod in this window and press the Options button that rests at the bottom right corner of the Portable Devices window, you'll be presented with the aptly named Options dialog box. It's within this dialog box that you'll find options for adding music to your iPod.

The Options dialog box

The Options dialog box is broken into four tabbed areas.

General tab

What a waste of a perfectly good tab. Other than providing a place to post MusicMatch Jukebox's product information, this area allows you to Reset those "Don't ask me again" messages so that, indeed, MusicMatch Jukebox *will* ask you again.

Audio tab

This tab is slightly more useful to iPod users. This area allows you to apply current digital sound enhancements to your files, apply volume leveling (a process that attempts to maintain a consistent volume among the songs on your iPod), and resample audio files encoded at more than a certain resolution (128kbps, for example) to be resampled to a different rate (files encoded at 160kbps will be resampled to 128kbps, for example).

Regrettably, only one of these options works on the Windows iPod. Sound enhancements such as EQ aren't copied to the iPod from a PC (though they are on a Mac) and you can't apply volume leveling to songs on the iPod (though you can apply volume leveling to files on the PC and then transfer them to the iPod).

However, if you select the resampling option, when you download songs to your iPod, they will be resampled to the settings you requested. This takes some time to do—about 45 seconds on a not-terribly-fast PC—so unless you're really pressed for space, don't bother using this option.

Synchronization tab

Ah, now we're cookin'. Settings in the Synchronization tab allow you to decide whether to synchronize your entire music library when you sync your iPod or just synchronize select playlists (**Figure 3.14**). This area also includes the "Automatically synchronize on device connection" option. With this option unchecked you can manually manage the contents of your iPod and mount your iPod on your PC without fear that its contents will be wiped out because the library on the PC doesn't match the songs on the iPod.

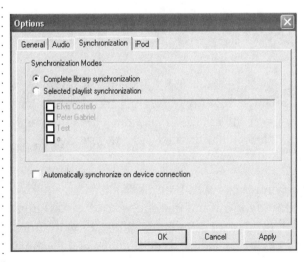

Figure 3.14
MusicMatch Jukebox's synchronization options.

iPod tab

And finally, the iPod area includes the options for automatically launching MusicMatch Jukebox when you plug the iPod into the PC, enabling FireWire disk use (where your iPod appears as a removable hard drive), and naming your iPod. You'll also find the iPod's version number in this portion of the Options window.

Moving music

If you've chosen to have your iPod updated whenever Music-Match Jukebox launches, all you need to do to move new songs to your iPod is plug it into your PC. MusicMatch Jukebox will launch and the songs in your library will be synchronized with the songs on your iPod. Even if you haven't chosen to update the iPod automatically, you can easily synchronize MusicMatch Jukebox's music library with your iPod by opening the Portable Devices window, selecting the iPod in the list to the left, and clicking the Sync button.

To add songs to your iPod when you've configured it to be updated manually, select your iPod in the Portable Devices window, open the My Library window, and drag the songs you want into the main window of the Portable Devices window. You can also drag and drop files from outside the program (from the Desktop or a window, for example) into the Portable Devices main window.

Finally, you can create playlists in the Playlists area of MusicMatch Jukebox's main window and click the Send button to move that playlist (and the music it includes) directly to your iPod.

Editing Track Tags

Editing track information in MusicMatch Jukebox is just as easy as carrying out a similar operation in iTunes. To produce the Edit Track Tag(s) window (**Figure 3.15**), just click the Tag button in the My Library window, right-click a track in your music library and select Edit Track Tag(s); or select a track, choose Music Library from the Options menu, and select the Edit Track Tag(s) command from the resulting submenu.

In this window you can enter such information as track title, track number, artist, album, genre, preference (akin to iTunes' Ratings), lyrics, notes, bios, tempo, and mood. You're welcome to knock yourself out filling in each field for every song in your library, but before you do, you should understand that the iPod will only use information entered in the Title, Artist, Album, and Genre fields.

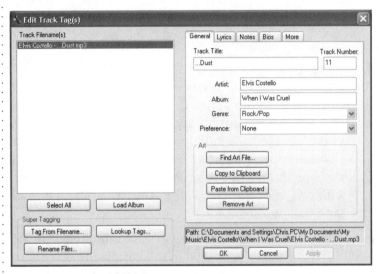

Figure 3.15 The Edit Track Tag(s) window.

This window offers some features not found in iTunes. Take the Load Album button, for example. I can best explain how this works by providing this for-instance: You've chosen to edit the track information for the Beatles' song "If I Fell." When you click the Load Album button, all the songs from the album *A Hard Days Night* appear in the Track Filename(s) list. If you were to then click the Select All button, you could edit tag information for all the songs on that album at one time.

In this window you'll also find options for looking up tags on the Internet (helpful if you've obtained music that hasn't already been tagged) and batch renaming selected files.

Other MusicMatch Jukebox Tricks

What other changes can you make in MusicMatch Jukebox that will effect your iPod?

- **Make volumes consistent.** If you scroll through your iPod's Settings screen you'll see the Sound Check option. This is a feature peculiar to the Macintosh version of the iPod and iTunes. When you switch Sound Check on in iTunes, the songs in the iTunes library are processed so that songs play at a consistent volume (some songs aren't wildly louder or softer than others). You can turn this effect on or off on the Macintosh iPod.

Although Sound Check appears in the Windows iPod's Settings screen, the feature isn't supported on that iPod. This doesn't mean, however, that you can't produce a similar effect in MusicMatch Jukebox.

In MusicMatch Jukebox this effect is produced with the Volume Leveling feature. Much like Sound Check, MusicMatch Jukebox will process songs in your music library so that they play at a volume similar to other Volume Leveling-processed songs. The difference between Sound Check and Volume Leveling is that you can't turn Volume Leveling off on the iPod. (Also, unlike in iTunes, you don't have to apply Volume Leveling to every song in your library. You can process a select group of songs.) Once the songs have been processed on the PC, that volume setting is maintained on the iPod, regardless of whether the Sound Check feature is turned on or off in the Settings screen.

To employ Volume Leveling, open the My Library window, select the songs you'd like to apply the effect to, and right-click a selected file. From the resulting contextual menu, select Prepare Track(s) for Volume Leveling. You can also invoke the Volume Leveling command in the Playlists window. Just select the songs you want to process in the playlists, right-click a selected file, and choose Prepare Track(s) for Volume Leveling from the contextual menu that appears.

- **Generate Random Playlists.** MusicMatch Jukebox includes the AutoDJ feature that generates playlists for you based on three criteria. It works this way:

Click the AutoDJ button in the My Library window and the AutoDJ window appears (**Figure 3.16**). In this window are three scrolling lists, each accompanied by a list of search criteria (album, artist, and genre, for example). To generate a random playlist, select different criteria in each list and enter the play time for the resulting playlist.

For example, if I chose by Album from the first list, AutoDJ would display all the albums in my library. I'd then check the albums I was willing to accept songs from. In the second list I might select by Artist. All the artists of the music in my library would appear in the list and I'd select those that I was willing to have appear in my playlist. And in the third list I might choose by Genre and select Jazz and Rock/Pop, thus ensuring that only jazz and rock/pop tunes would appear in my playlist.

I'd then enter a playtime of three hours and click the Get Tracks button to generate the playlist. AutoDJ would grab three hours-worth of songs from my library that met my criteria and randomly place their titles in MusicMatch Jukebox's Playlists window. I could then save that playlist and later transfer it to my iPod.

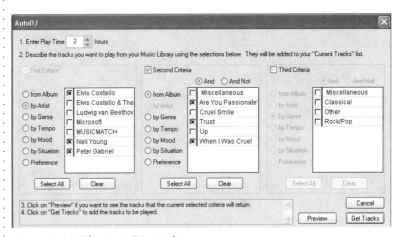

Figure 3.16 The AutoDJ window.

Software Alternatives

Although the Windows iPod ships with MusicMatch Jukebox, it's not your only option for moving songs to your iPod. Two other fine applications that were originally designed to allow Macintosh iPods to function with Windows PCs now also work with the Windows iPod. Those two utilities are Mediafour's (*www.mediafour.com*) $30 XPlay and Joe Masters' free EphPod (*www.ephpod.com*).

XPlay

Mediafour is known among Mac users primarily for its Mac-Drive product, which allows Mac volumes to be viewed and manipulated on a PC running Microsoft Windows. In January 2002, the company held a press briefing for a product called XPod, claiming that the product would give Windows users the same kind of access to the iPod that Mac users have.

Somewhere along the way, Apple suggested that the name *XPod* was a little too close to *iPod*, and Mediafour obligingly changed the name to XPlay. Though the name had changed, the product's capabilities did not. The betas of XPlay released in the spring of 2002 showed a program with a lot of promise: the capability to mount and manipulate the iPod as an external drive on the Desktop or through Windows Explorer, the option to have Windows Media Player 7.x and later recognize the iPod as a portable music player (letting you see and play the music on the iPod, as well as copy music from Windows Media Player to the iPod), and the capability to update your iPod's music files automatically when the iPod is attached to the PC.

Now in final form, XPlay lives up to its promise, providing those with both Mac and Windows' iPods a way to use their portable players with Windows Media Player.

Installing and configuring XPlay

Follow these steps to set up XPlay on your PC:

1. On a PC running Windows 98SE, ME, 2000, or XP, install XPlay.

2. Restart your PC.

3. When the PC is fully booted, plug your iPod into the PC with a FireWire cable.

   Your iPod will mount as a removable drive (**Figures 3.17** and **3.18**), and a small icon will appear in the Task Bar. (When you click this icon, you can unmount the iPod.) In short order, the XPlay iPod Setup Wizard appears.

4. Click Next to begin the setup process.

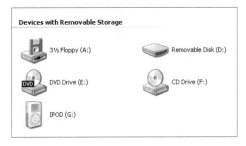

Figure 3.17
The iPod as a removable drive.

Figure 3.18
The contents of the drive are as accessible to your PC as any other removable drive.

5. In the first screen, change your iPod's name, if you want (**Figure 3.19**), and click Next.

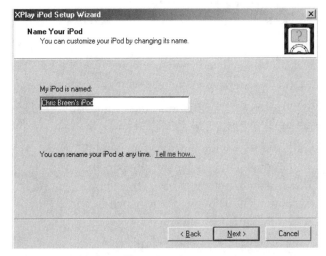

Figure 3.19 XPlay offers you the option to rename your iPod.

In the resulting synchronization option screen, specify whether you'd like the iPod to be updated automatically when you plug it in or whether you want to update the iPod yourself (**Figure 3.20**).

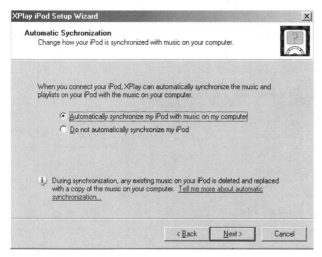

Figure 3.20 Choose your synchronization options in XPlay's Setup Wizard.

6. Make your choice, and click Next.

   Next, you are asked to select a music collection to synchronize with: Windows Media Player or a folder of your choosing. Which you choose depends largely on where you have your music stored on your PC. If it's already in Windows Media Player, choose this option. If you've dropped your music into a folder on your PC somewhere, you may prefer to synchronize to that folder.

7. Make your choice, and click Next.

   In the next screen, you're offered the option to register your iPod with Apple; XPlay will launch your Web browser and take you to Apple's Registration site. If you haven't already registered your iPod, feel free to register it this way. You don't have to register for XPlay to work, however.

8. Again, make your choice, and click Next to complete the setup process.

   XPlay and your iPod are ready to use.

If you'd like to change the way that XPlay is set up later—to update your iPod manually rather than have it updated automatically, for example—right-click the XPlay icon in Windows' Notification area, and choose Change Synchronization Options from the contextual menu (**Figure 3.21**). Choosing this command walks you through the latter part of the XPlay setup process.

Figure 3.21
Select this command to launch XPlay's Setup application.

Playing with XPlay

XPlay offers you two ways to get to the music on your iPod: by browsing the items inside the XPlay folder that XPlay places on your iPod or by going through the default media player. In this section, I'll look at both methods.

When you finish the XPlay setup, the installer places an XPlay music folder at the root level of your iPod. The contents of this folder are arranged similarly to the iPod interface. Inside the XPlay music folder, you'll find:

- **Albums.** Inside the Albums folder, you'll find a list of all the albums on your iPod (**Figure 3.22**), as well as another folder called (all songs on all albums). Opening this folder reveals—as you might expect—all the songs on all the albums on your iPod.

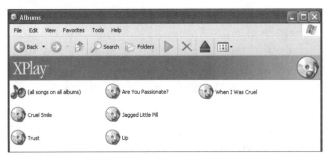

Figure 3.22 The contents of XPlay's Albums folder.

- **Artists.** Here, you'll see file icons that represent all the artists on your iPod. Double-click an artist folder, and you'll spy another folder called (all songs by "artist"), in which "artist" is the name of the artist. For example, clicking on the James Brown folder, you'll see another folder called (all songs by James Brown). Double-click this folder, and you'll see a list of all the songs on your iPod by that artist—"Prisoner of Love," "Papa's Got a Brand New Bag," and "I Got the Feelin,'" for example. Inside an individual artist's folder, you'll also see the artist's songs broken down by albums—"Can Your Heart Stand It!!" and "Ain't That a Groove," for example. Finally, the Artist folder contains the (all songs by all artists) folder that... well, you can probably guess.

- **Playlists.** This folder contains all the playlists on your iPod. Double-clicking a playlist reveals all the files within that playlist.

- **Songs.** Double-click this folder to display all the songs on your iPod.

- **XPlay Help.** Double-click this file to view XPlay's help file.

Copying via drag and drop

Using this hierarchy, you can easily add audio files to your iPod by dragging them from a drive on your PC to a folder on the iPod that contains songs.

Note that this drag-and-drop copying scheme works in one direction only. Mediafour respects Apple's desire that you not copy files from the iPod to your computer. If you attempt to copy a song from one of the XPlay folders to your PC's hard drive, you'll see a warning message telling you that this practice is a no-no. You can copy a shortcut of the file to your hard drive, if you like, but when you double-click that alias, the file will play only if the iPod is mounted and that file exists on the iPod.

File Ripping and Windows

One feature not found in XPlay and EphPod is the ability to rip music files from audio discs. Thankfully, this isn't necessary since you have a copy of MusicMatch Jukebox. But those of you Mac users reading this chapter in the hope of using your Mac iPod with Windows are in for a slight shock when you attempt to rip an audio CD with Windows Media Player.

Yes, you can shove an audio CD into your PC and ask Windows Media Player to extract the audio files from that CD, and the application will oblige. Regrettably for you as an iPod owner, the form that those extracted files take are not compatible with your iPod. Windows Media Player encodes files in a format that's friendly only to Windows Media Player. If you try to copy such files to your iPod, you'll receive an error message indicating that the iPod can accept only MP3, AIFF, and WAV files.

If you want to extract audio files from a CD in a format that the iPod can understand, you'll have to use MusicMatch Jukebox or a utility such as FreeRIP (**www.mgshareware.com**).

Copying via Windows Media Player

If you've chosen to use Windows Media Player in conjunction with XPlay, follow these steps to copy songs from your PC to the iPod.

1. Launch a copy of Windows Media Player.

2. Click the copy to CD or Device button. The main Windows Media Player window will split in two, with the left side devoted to files on your PC and the right side devoted to files on your iPod (**Figure 3.23**). If your iPod doesn't appear in the list to the right, select it from the device list pop-up menu above the right pane in the Windows Media Player window.

    After churning away for awhile, Windows Media Player displays all the songs on your iPod.

3. If you want to play files on your iPod from Windows Media Player, return to the XPlay music folder on your iPod, navigate to a song or playlist you want to play, right-click that item, and select Play from the contextual menu.

Regrettably, you can't play the songs in the list by double-clicking the song title; neither can you copy the songs back to your PC.

Figure 3.23 The iPod as a portable player in Windows Media Player.

Note that the files on your iPod must be configured to play with Windows Media Player. Invariably when you install a new Windows multimedia application it wants control of your PC's media files. MusicMatch Jukebox is no exception. Unless, during installation, you tell it not to take charge of all the MP3 files on your PC and iPod, those files will play in MusicMatch Jukebox when you double-click them.

If you'd like XPlay's files to play in Windows Media Player but they insist on opening in MusicMatch Jukebox, open Windows Media Player and select Options from the Tools menu. Click the File Types tab and, in the File types scrolling window, check MP3 Format Sound (**Figure 3.24**). Click Apply to direct MP3 files to play in Windows Media Player.

Figure 3.24
Configuring Windows
Media Player to play
media files.

4. To copy songs from your PC to the iPod, select a
compatible music file (MP3, AIFF, or WAV) from the
left pane in Windows Media Player, and click the
Copy Music button.

The song will be copied to your iPod. If you try to
copy a song in any other format (Windows Media
format, for example), the song title will turn red and,
in the status column, you'll see an entry that reads
"An Error Occurred." (At this point you're welcome
to thank Microsoft for developing proprietary standards that fail to work with non-Microsoft products.)

EphPod 2

Joe Masters' EphPod 2 is a free application that allows you to
manage the music on your iPod. Like MusicMatch Jukebox, it
lets you move files to the iPod from Windows, launch songs
in the designated media player (Windows Media Player or
MusicMatch Jukebox, for example), and create contacts and
calendar events. EphPod uses a spreadsheet-style columned
interface to represent the layers of the iPod, rather than XPlay's
folders. Unlike XPlay, EphPod does most of the work inter-
nally, rather than through Windows Explorer or Windows
Media Player.

Setting up EphPod

EphPod requires that your PC be running Windows 98SE, ME, NT, 2000, or XP. If you're running Windows 98SE, you may want to search for upgraded FireWire drivers or upgrade your version of Windows before you start. Then follow these steps to make EphPod work for you:

1. EphPod works perfectly well with the Windows iPod. If you'd like it to work with a Macintosh iPod (the purpose for which it was originally designed), you need to install an application that allows the PC to "see" the Mac iPod.

   XPlay uses Mediafour's own MacDrive for this purpose—and EphPod can, too—but EphPod's creator has had better success with DataViz's $40 MacOpener. Mr. Masters offers a version of EphPod that contains a 15-day trial version of MacOpener so you can try it for yourself. You can find this version at *www.ephpod.com/download.html.*

2. Install EphPod.

3. Connect your iPod to the PC with a FireWire cable.

4. Launch EphPod.

   The EphPod Installation Wizard starts. You don't have much to do other than click a Next button if your iPod is attached and recognized by the PC. (You can tell that the iPod is recognized if it appears as a removable drive.) During the setup process, EphPod creates a database of all the songs, playlists, artists, and albums on your iPod's hard drive.

Using EphPod

EphPod's interface is similar to Windows Explorer (**Figure 3.25**). The top half of the EphPod window—called iPod View—is divided into panes that represent navigation layers on the iPod. The bottom half of the window—called Songs—lists songs. Navigating through EphPod is a simple matter of choosing entries in the iPod View section, selecting subentries in the second and third panes, and then selecting songs in the song list in the bottom half of the window.

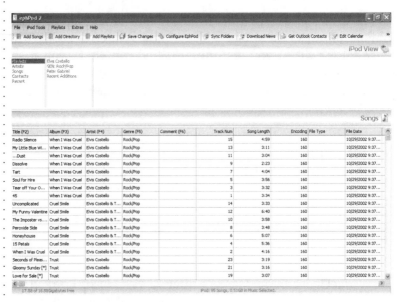

Figure 3.25 EphPod's interface.

In the first pane at the top of the window, you'll find entries for Playlists, Artists, Songs, Contacts, and Recent. These entries work this way:

- Click the Playlists entry, and the playlists on your iPod appear in the second column. Click a playlist, and the songs in the playlist appear in the third column. Double-click a title in the third column, and the song list scrolls to the point where that song appears at the top of the song list.

- Click the Artists entry in the first column, and the second column reveals all the artists on your iPod in the second column. Click an artist, and that artist's albums appear in the third column. Click the All entry in the second column, and all the albums on your iPod appear in the third column. Click an album in the third column, and all the songs on that album appear in the song list.

- Click the Songs entry in the first column, and all the songs on the iPod appear in the song list. You can sort songs by several factors, including Title, Artist, Album, Genre, Comment, Track Number, Song Length, Encoding (the song's bit rate), File Type (MPEG, AIFF, or WAV), File Date, File Size, File Name (the path to the file), and

Song ID (the number assigned to the song in EphPod's database).

- Click the Contacts entry, and the subject headings for all your contacts appear in the second column. If you double-click a contact, the Contact Information Window appears. You can edit that information in this window.

To play a song in EphPod, double-click its title in the song list to launch the default media player and play the song. To load all the songs in a playlist into the default media player (**Figure 3.26**), right-click a playlist, and choose Play Playlist from the resulting contextual menu (**Figure 3.27**).

Figure 3.26 A playlist playing in Windows Media Player.

Add Playlist from File	Ctrl+P
New Playlist	Ctrl+N
Delete Selected	Del
Rename Selected Playlist	
Delete All Playlists	Ctrl+D
Sort By Name	
Play Playlist	

Figure 3.27
Right-click a playlist to play all the songs in the default media player.

Transferring music with EphPod

EphPod helps you move audio files on and off the iPod. Here's how to do so:

1. From EphPod's File menu, choose Add Songs (**Figure 3.28**).

   The Select Songs dialog box opens.

Figure 3.28
EphPod's Add Songs command.

2. Navigate to a folder that contains MP3 files you'd like to add to your iPod.

   Note that EphPod doesn't allow you to add AIFF files to the iPod, but does support WAV files. Also unlike MusicMatch Jukebox, it does support Audible.com files (or should, by the time you read this). That's right, although Apple claims that Audible.com files are not compatible with the Windows version of the iPod, what Apple really means is that the *software* bundled with the iPod isn't compatible with Audible.com files. EphPod makes it possible to play these files on your Windows iPod (see "Audible.com and EphPod").

3. Control-click to select more than one file, and click Open. The Writing Songs window appears, displaying the progress of the copy (**Figure 3.29**). This window disappears when the copy is complete.

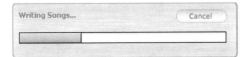

Figure 3.29
Making progress.

Alternatively, you can choose the Add Songs From Directory command from the File menu and add songs through a Windows Explorer interface.

Audible.com and EphPod

For those Windows iPod users who've skipped directly to this chapter, I should mention that the Mac iPod is capable of playing electronic books produced and sold by Audible.com. By default, the Windows iPod can not play Audible.com files.

As this book goes to press, however, EphPod's creator, Joe Masters, is in the final stages of securing a deal with Audible.com that will allow you to play Audible.com files on your Windows iPod. My sincere hope is that by the time you read this, the Audible.com-compatible version of EphPod will be ready.

To add Audible.com files to your Windows iPod, follow these steps:

1. Using Audible Manager (Audible.com's Windows application for managing its audio files), download an audible file in format 2, 3, or 4 (the iPod doesn't support format 1 files).

2. Launch EphPod and choose Add Song from its File menu.

3. Locate the .aa file that corresponds to the audible file you've downloaded (this is usually found by following this path: files\audible\programs\downloads\).

4. Select the File and click Open.

The file appears in EphPod, ready to be downloaded to your iPod.

Note that if your iPod is Windows-formatted (with iPod firmware versions 1.2.2 and below), it will lose the audible bookmarks when you connect the iPod to another computer or when you manually reset the iPod. If your iPod is formatted for the Mac, those bookmarks remain. This is due to the fact that the Mac iPod updates a file on its hard drive called Play Counts whenever it is turned off. (This Play Counts file keeps track of not only how many times you've played a song on your iPod but also Audible.com bookmarks.) A Windows-formatted iPod also carries this Play Counts file, but fails to update the file correctly.

Using EphPod's other options

EphPod has its own unique features, including these:

- **Contact creation.** As this book goes to press, not even iTunes can do this. For more information on how to create contacts in EphPod, see Chapter 5.

- **Calendar Editor.** EphPod includes a feature for editing vCalendar files on your iPod. For more information on this feature and other calendar related iPod functions, see Chapter 6.

- **Memo creation.** This is another not-yet-done-in-iTunes feature. Choose New Memo (As Contact) from the File menu, and a window appears where you can put down your most personal thoughts (or, perhaps, your grocery list). For those who are interested in such things, EphPod places your memo in the vCard's Title field.

- **The option to create playlists from a variety of sources.** From the Playlists menu, you can create playlists based on album title, genre, all songs, or orphan songs (songs that aren't associated with a particular album).

- **Copy Songs to Directory.** Then there's a feature guaranteed to pique the interest of those on both sides of the music-piracy fence. When you right-click a song or group of selected songs in the song list, you'll see the Copy Song to Directory command in the resulting contextual menu (**Figure 3.30**). When you invoke this command, you can copy files *from* the iPod *to* the PC. If you chose to, you could lug your iPod to a PC-packing friend's house and copy songs from your iPod onto your friend's PC. This practice would go against Apple's "Don't steal music" admonition, however.

Figure 3.30
EphPod allows you to copy songs from your iPod to your PC.

- **Download news.** New to EphPod is the ability to download news stories from such sources as BBC World News, CNET News.com, and SlashDot (**Figure 3.31**). You can also download local weather forecasts. To configure such downloads, select Configuration from the Extras menu, and click the Download Options tab.

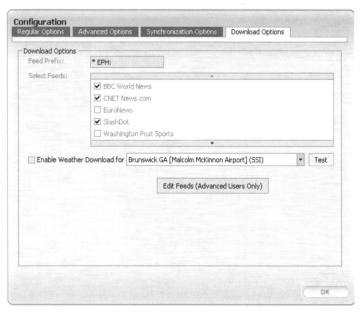

Figure 3.31 EphPod's news service option.

Why Use a Third-Party Application?

Given that MusicMatch Jukebox is included with the Windows version of the iPod and Macintosh iPod owners can convert their iPod's into Windows compatible devices by downloading Apple's iPod Software Updater for Windows and MusicMatch Jukebox (the non-pro version), why bother with XPlay or EphPod?

To begin with, MusicMatch Jukebox's interface is a little cluttered and sometimes difficult to navigate. Both XPlay and EphPod allow you to use Windows Media Player, an application you may be more comfortable with.

continues on next page

Why Use a Third-Party Application? *continued*

If you're a Mac iPod user looking for a way to use your iPod on a PC without reformatting the iPod's hard drive, XPlay is an attractive option. Unlike EphPod, XPlay includes the software necessary for a Windows PC to mount and use a Mac iPod. Mac iPod owners must purchase a separate utility (at $10 more than the price of XPlay) to use their iPods with EphPod.

EphPod is an enticing alternative not only because it's free, but because of all the things it can do that MusicMatch Jukebox can't: create contacts, edit calendars, download news headlines, copy songs from the iPod to your PC's hard drive, and play Audible.com files (and download them to your iPod). This is rich set of features—some of which aren't found even in iTunes.

The Removable Drive

Given the praise heaped upon the iPod for its musical capabilities, it's easy to overlook the fact that it's more than a music player equipped with a hard drive. The iPod is also a capable FireWire drive that happens to play music. This distinction may not seem terribly important until the day you're sitting in front of an Apple PowerBook whose hard drive has suddenly gone south while your co-workers—many of whom have flown in from overseas—anxiously await the now-vanished PowerPoint presentation you slaved over for the past six weeks.

If you'd set aside a portion of your iPod for a system capable of booting your Mac and a teensy bit more room for a copy of PowerPoint and that presentation, what could have been a disaster would turn into an opportunity to demonstrate why you're more deserving of an executive parking space than that schlep Henderson, who smells of garlic and routinely pinches your yogurt from the office mini-fridge.

And although Windows users can't boot their PCs from an iPod, the iPod can still serve as a useful backup and storage solution for those who are not running the Mac OS.

In this chapter, I'll show you how the iPod operates as an external storage device, how you can exploit it in this regard, and—yes—how to move music off your iPod and onto all the computers you own (and discuss the moral ramifications of doing so).

FireWire to Go

When Apple introduced its fast serial input/output technology, FireWire, it didn't do so by hailing the benefits of this technology as they might relate to video and audio applications. Rather, Steve Jobs demonstrated FireWire by plugging a small hard drive into a Mac. What's the big deal?

To begin with, the hard drive wasn't powered. Second, the Mac was.

Again, *what's the big deal?*

Before this, external hard drives—most of which used the Small Computer System Interface (SCSI) technology—had to be plugged into an electrical source. And the computer intended for use with this SCSI drive had to be powered off when you plugged the SCSI device into it. Otherwise, you were possibly in for a heap of trouble—trouble that might include a corrupted hard drive or a fried motherboard on your computer.

This FireWire stuff was remarkable because it could pull power from the device it was plugged into via the FireWire cable, and you could plug and unplug devices with the drive and computer switched on—a process known as *hot swapping.*

This trip down memory lane serves to explain that because the iPod is, in essence, a FireWire drive with a few components thrown in (okay, *elegantly* thrown in) to make it play music, it operates in a similar fashion to any other FireWire drive. Just like some other FireWire drives, the iPod doesn't require external power when it's plugged into a computer. Just like other FireWire drives, an iPod can be plugged into a running computer, and (if you've configured the iPod to mount as a FireWire drive, as I suggested in Chapters 2 and 3) you have a reasonable expectation that its icon will appear shortly on your Mac's Desktop or within Windows' My Computer window.

As I mentioned earlier, the iPod can't be used to boot a PC. This is a limitation of the Windows operating system, not of the iPod, so if you feel shortchanged as a Windows user, please direct any testy letters to Redmond rather than to Cupertino. Because the iPod can't boot a PC, my Windows readers may feel a little left out in the early part of the chapter. For this,

I apologize, but I promise to deliver a few Windows-centric tips later in the proceedings.

The iPod can, however, boot a Mac—meaning that the hard drive inside the iPod can start up your Mac if your Mac supports being booted from a FireWire drive. (The Blue & White Power Mac G3 and Power Mac G4 [PCI Graphics] don't support FireWire booting.) This feat may not seem so remarkable until you try the same trick with another FireWire drive that doesn't support booting.

There's no trick to getting an iPod to boot your Mac. Plug it in, designate the iPod as the startup device, and restart your computer. The trick is installing a bootable operating system on the iPod. With Mac OS 9, this is no big deal—Mac OS 9 installs as you'd expect. And in early versions of Mac OS X, this was also a nearly painless process. But Mac OS X 10.2 (Jaguar) has made installing OS X on an iPod a bit more challenging (though not impossible). In the next few pages, I'll show you how to place each of these operating systems on your iPod and, when they're in place, how to boot into them.

Installing the Mac OS on your iPod

Placing Mac OS 9 and versions of Mac OS X before Mac OS X 10.2 on your iPod is remarkably similar to configuring any Mac's hard drive as a startup disk. To start, just plug your iPod into a Mac running either Mac OS 9 or Mac OS X.

If the iPod's icon doesn't appear on the Desktop, launch iTunes 2 or iTunes 3, click the iPod in the Source list, click the iPod Preferences button at the bottom of the iTunes window, and select Enable FireWire Disk Use in the resulting iPod Preferences window. Then quit iTunes.

Insert a Mac OS installation disc into your Mac's CD/DVD drive. Note that a Software Restore CD won't allow you to install a copy of the Mac OS on your iPod. You must have a separate installer disc, such as the Mac OS 9 or Mac OS X 10.1x installation disc.

Now I'll show you the steps for installing Mac OS 9 and Mac OS X 10.1.x.

Note that throughout this section, I refer to Mac OS X 10.1.x. I do this to distinguish this earlier version of Mac OS X from the later 10.2.x (Jaguar release). Anytime I refer to Mac OS X 10.1.x, you can assume I'm also referring to earlier versions of Mac OS X. I specifically mention 10.1.x because, quite frankly, any earlier versions of Mac OS X were pretty marginal. If you haven't upgraded Mac OS X to at least 10.1, you should.

Installing Mac OS 9

Just follow these steps to install Mac OS 9 on your iPod:

1. Insert the Mac OS 9 CD, and choose Restart from the Special menu.

2. As soon as you hear the Mac's startup sound, press and hold down the keyboard's C key.

3. When you see the happy Mac face, let go of the C key.

   Now the Mac is booting from the CD-ROM you inserted. The CD window should open, revealing the Mac OS Install application.

4. Double-click this application to launch the installer.

5. Click the Continue button in the resulting Welcome screen.

6. In the Destination screen that appears next, choose your iPod from the Destination Disk pop-up menu (**Figure 4.1**); then click Select.

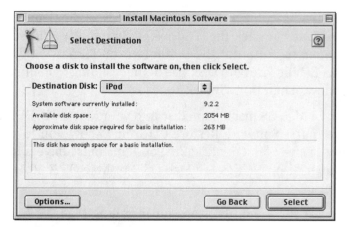

Figure 4.1 Select your iPod in the Mac OS 9 Installer's Destination screen.

7. Click through the Important Information and License Agreement screens after reading every word in them carefully.

I'm kidding. No one reads these things. But agree to the license agreement, because if you don't, the installer quits, and then where are you?

8. Click Start in the Install Macintosh Software screen to begin the installation (**Figure 4.2**).

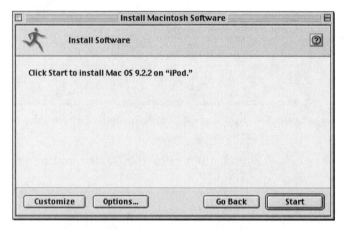

Figure 4.2 Click Start to begin the installation.

9. Go have a cup of coffee; the installation takes a while (**Figure 4.3**).

Figure 4.3 Sixteen minutes is plenty of time to get a cup of coffee while your Mac creates an iPod you can boot from.

10. When the installer is finished, click Quit.

11. Choose Control Panels and then Startup Disk from the Apple menu (**Figure 4.4**).

Your iPod appears as one of the startup-disk choices.

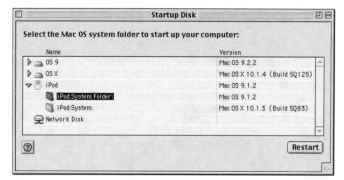

Figure 4.4 The Mac OS, cozily tucked away on your iPod.

12. Click the iPod; then click the Restart button to boot from your iPod.

Installing Mac OS X 10.1.x

And to install Mac OS X 10.1.x on your iPod, follow these instructions:

1. Insert the Mac OS X Installer disc.

2. Either restart your Mac and hold down the C key to boot from the Installer disc or double-click the Install Mac OS X application on the CD.

3. Click the Restart button in the resulting Install Mac OS X window.

The Mac will restart and boot from the OS X Installer disc.

4. When the installer appears, select the language you'd like your Mac to use, and click Continue.

5. In the Welcome screen, click Continue again.

6. Click through the Important Information and License Agreement screens after memorizing every word in them (yeah, right...).

Agree to the license agreement because if you don't... well, you know.

7. In the Select a Destination screen, select your iPod, and click Continue.

    In this screen, you'll see the option to erase your hard drive and format it as either a Mac OS Extended or Unix File System volume. *Do not select this option.* It will not only erase every bit of information on your drive (including all the songs on your iPod), but also may cause your iPod to stop working until you reset it with the iMac Software Updater. (See Chapter 8 for information on troubleshooting your iPod.)

8. In the next Easy Install screen, specify whether you want to proceed with the installation as is or perform a customized installation.

    Because you want both a bootable iPod and one on which you can store as much music as possible, click the Customize button.

9. In the Custom Install screen that results, select only the language options that you're likely to use.

    These languages take up space on your iPod's hard drive that could be devoted to storing tunes.

10. Click Install, and go have two cups of coffee; this installation takes longer than the Mac OS 9 installation.

11. When the installation is complete, click Restart.

    Don't worry if you're not around to click Restart; the Mac will restart on its own 30 seconds after the installation is complete. Your Mac will boot into Mac OS X 10.1.x from your iPod.

12. When the Mac reboots, go through the Mac OS X setup procedure.

    When you finally get to the Desktop, Software Update will launch automatically. Mac OS X gets better with each update, and it's likely that a few updates are waiting for you.

13. If Software Update discovers updates, install them
(**Figure 4.5**).

Figure 4.5 Software updates undoubtedly await you.

14. After the updates are installed, restart (if necessary),
and run Software Update again.

Certain updates become available to System Update
only when other updates are installed. This situation
used to be a real inconvenience that required you to
install—separately—one update after another. Apple
has lately ganged groups of these updates into a single
installation package, such as the Mac OS X Update
Combo 10.1.5. Such dependent installations haven't
disappeared completely—and who knows what the
future might hold—so it's a good idea to run System
Update a couple of times in a row to be sure that
you've got all the latest updates.

Your iPod is ready to boot your Mac into Mac OS X 10.1.x.

Installing Mac OS X 10.2.x (Jaguar)

A reader of the first edition of the book wrote in to say that, following the instructions of the book, he was unable to install Mac OS X 10.2 on his iPod. What did I—"Mr. Secrets of the iPod," as he put it—have to say on the subject? Just this:

As you've observed, using the Mac OS X 10.2 installer, you cannot place a bootable copy of Mac OS X on your iPod. When I attempted to do so, the OS X installer got as far as installing the contents of the first installation disc (there are two installation discs), and the iPod refused to boot to allow the installation of the second disc.

But because I am "Mr. Secrets of the iPod," allow me to let you in on this little secret: You can install a copy of Mac OS X 10.2.x on your iPod, and your iPod will boot from it. The trick is that you must move an existing copy of Mac OS X 10.2.x from your Mac's hard drive to the iPod. To do this, I use Mike Bombich's $5 Carbon Copy Cloner (*www.bombich.com/software/ccc.html*)—a utility that "clones" a Mac OS X installation from one volume to another and allows you to make that cloned volume bootable. Here's how to go about it:

1. With your iPod configured as a FireWire drive, plug it into your Mac.

    The iPod's icon will appear on the Desktop (or, if Finder Preferences aren't configured to display hard drives on the Desktop, in the Computer window).

2. Download, install, and launch a copy of Carbon Copy Cloner.

    Version 1.4 and later versions are compatible with Mac OS X 10.2.x.

3. From the Source Disk pop-up menu in the Cloning Console window, choose a volume on your Mac that contains Mac OS X 10.1.2.x.

    Although Carbon Copy Cloner allows you to select which items at the root level of your OS X volume you want to clone, it doesn't allow you to choose files and folders within those root-level items. In other words, you can't tell Carbon Copy Cloner to clone only one or two applications within the Applications folder. You either clone the entire Applications folder (and all its contents) or none of the Applications folder.

For this reason, it's a good idea to clone an OS X 10.2 volume that isn't packed with extra files and applications. Cloning an 8.8 GB OS X 10.2 volume to your 10 GB iPod will leave you precious little space for songs, contacts, and calendars.

4. Choose your iPod from the Target Disk pop-up menu.

5. Command-click the items in the Items to be Copied list that you *don't* want to clone to your iPod (**Figure 4.6**).

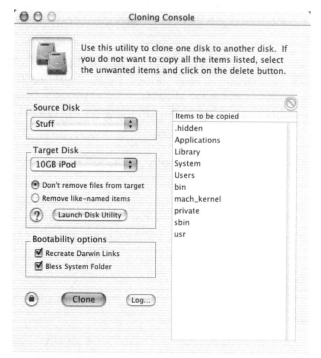

Figure 4.6 Use Carbon Copy Cloner to create a bootable iPod running Mac OS X 10.2.

Items that you should copy to create a bootable (and useful) startup disk include:

- .hidden
- Applications
- Library
- System
- Users

- bin
- mach.kernel
- private
- sbin
- usr

6. Click the Remove button (just above the Items to be Copied list) to exclude the selected files from the cloning process.

7. In the Bootability Options section of the window, make sure that both the Recreate Darwin Links and Bless System Folder check boxes are checked.

8. Click the Lock icon, and enter your user name and password when you're requested to do so.

9. Click the Clone button to begin cloning the source volume to your iPod.

10. When the process is complete, quit Carbon Copy Cloner, choose System Preferences from the Apple menu, and click the Startup Disk system preference.

   Your iPod will appear in the list of bootable volumes.

11. Click the iPod's System folder and click Restart to boot from your iPod.

Why Create a Bootable iPod?

After reading through the last few pages, you may wonder why you'd bother to install Mac OS 9 or Mac OS X (or both) on your iPod. The truth is, you may not need to. You may own the one Macintosh in the world that will never, ever suffer from hard-disk corruption, extension conflicts, and buggy software. For you, having a reliable bootup disk that contains all your troubleshooting utilities isn't necessary.

Or your musical cravings may be so intense that if you can't cram every minute of the 264 hours of music that the 20 GB iPod is capable of storing onto your iPod, you'll wind up with a bad case of the heebie-jeebies (or, worse yet, the jim-jams).

continues on next page

Why Create a Bootable iPod? *continued*

I'm not one of these people. Because I troubleshoot Macs for a living, I find the ability to store all the tools I need on such a portable bootable hard drive to be a real boon. And although I love music, I hardly find it limiting to store only 30 hours of music on my iPod. It's so easy to replace songs on the device with new material that when I get bored with my current selections, I spend a couple of hours transferring a different 30 CDs to my iPod, and my listening needs are met for the next month.

Additional data storage

Being able to boot your Macintosh from an iPod is a good first step, but it's only a first step. To make your iPod both bootable and useful, consider using its data-storage capabilities for the following purposes:

- **Installing your troubleshooting utilities.** The most important reason for making a bootable iPod is that it allows you to repair the hard drive that *should* be booting your Mac. If your Mac's hard drive is on the fritz and won't boot your Mac, it's a godsend to have another hard drive that can boot your Mac and contains all your troubleshooting utilities. Currently, those utilities might include Disk Warrior from Alsoft (*www.alsoft.com*), a splendid tool for repairing low-level corruption; TechTool Pro from Micromat (*www.micromat.com*); and Norton Utilities from Symantec (*www.symantec.com*).

  As this book goes to press, all three utilities are capable of troubleshooting and repairing both Mac OS 9 and Mac OS X disks, but the only one that can run from a disk running Mac OS X is Norton Utilities. For this reason, if you have multiple repair utilities (not a bad idea, considering that each has its strengths), install Mac OS 9 on your iPod and run your utilities from this older Apple operating system.

  Note that as of January 2003, Apple has pounded the final nail into Mac OS 9's coffin. Macs released after 1/2003 will be unable to boot from a Mac OS 9 volume. Should you own one of these Macs, there's no point in installing Mac OS 9 on your iPod unless you intend to use it to boot pre-2003 Macs.

- **Macintosh: Keeping applications you need close at hand.** If it's your job to chair the next meeting, and you absolutely need a PowerPoint presentation to make that meeting a success, install not only a copy of your presentation on the iPod, but a working copy of PowerPoint as well.

- **Macintosh: Keeping drivers and accessories you need close at hand.** Fat lot of good it does you to boot from your iPod, fire up your graphing application, and then not be able to print that all-important flow chart because your iPod doesn't have a copy of the driver that allows it to use the company printer.

- **Keeping network settings, serial numbers, and passwords close at hand.** When you configure your iPod as an external drive, configure it fully. Nothing is more frustrating than being unable to get on the Internet because you've neglected to configure your network settings. Likewise, it's all well and good that you've installed Applications X, Y, and Z on your iPod, but if you haven't run them and entered the serial numbers that allow them to function, you could be up a creek when you're on the road and don't have those serial numbers at hand.

- **Macintosh and PC: Taking your user folder with you.** Under Mac OS X and Windows XP, your user folder holds most of your computing life: your Documents folder, music files, pictures, movies, network settings, the works. If you keep a copy of your user folder on your iPod, copy that folder to a Mac running Mac OS X or a PC running Windows XP, create a new user on that computer, and copy the information from your user folder to that new user, you've got a configuration darned close to the computer at home or work.

- **Macintosh and PC: Keeping a backup of important documents.** If you're working on something that you absolutely can't afford to lose—the company's yearly financial statement, your term paper, or the digital movie of your daughter's first birthday—keep a backup copy on your iPod. It's also worthwhile to keep a backup of your Address Book data, emails you might need to refer to, and your Web-browser bookmarks.

It's not necessary to keep a copy of absolutely everything on your computer—just those few items that will make you tear your hair out if they're missing.

- **PC: Transferring your files and settings.** You can select the iPod as a destination for files and settings transferred with Windows XP's Files and Settings Transfer Wizard. (To access this wizard, open the Start menu and follow this path: All Programs > Accessories > System Tools > Files and Settings Transfer Wizard.)

  Just run the wizard, select the iPod as the destination disk, and let Windows copy your files and settings to the iPod. If you need to restore those files to your PC or transfer them to another PC, run the Files and Settings Transfer Wizard once again, select your iPod as the source disk, and copy the files to the PC.

The Hidden Revealed: Song Storage on the iPod

If you mount your iPod as an external storage device and double-click its icon, you'll be surprised to find that it contains no more than two folders: Contacts and Calendars. You know that the iPod contains your entire library of Kate Bush CDs, yet they're nowhere to be seen. Has Apple created a stealth partition that stores only song data? Do the songs sit in some kind of temporary storage buffer and disappear when the battery drains? Is the iPod really some remarkable wireless receiving device that plays songs beamed from Apple's super-secret orbiting satellite?

No, no, and no.

Apple has done no more than create a scheme whereby the iPod's music files are placed in an invisible folder. Those music files sit right alongside the Contacts and Calendars folders; you just can't see them.

Why would Apple do such a thing? Simple: to make it harder to copy files from your iPod to a Macintosh or PC.

And why would Apple want to discourage such a procedure? Because Apple doesn't want the iPod to be a device that facilitates the practice of sharing music illegally. Leaving these files out in the open could tempt people who would not otherwise pirate music, and it might leave Apple open to criticism (and lawsuits) from the stodgier elements of the entertainment industry.

If this is the case, why didn't Apple come up with some impossible-to-crack encryption system, rather than this invisibility scheme? I'll let Apple's CEO, Steve Jobs, answer that one:

"Piracy is not a technological issue. It's a behavior issue."

If I may be so bold as to interpret Mr. Jobs' words, I believe he's saying that no matter how secure the knot you tie is, someone will come along and untie it. And he's correct. Countless bright individuals take it as a personal challenge to outwit any copy-protection scheme that comes along. Those who are bent on piracy will always find a way to defeat any copy-protection scheme they encounter. And because copy-protection schemes *will* be defeated, companies that embrace copy protection risk creating an expensive and time-consuming cycle of devising protection schemes, waiting for them to be broken, devising new protection schemes, waiting for *them* to be broken, and on, and on, and on.

Apple decided that it didn't care to jump aboard this merry-go-round. Parties that have a greater stake in the game—the recording industry, for example—could spend their time and money on copy-protection schemes and Washington lobbyists. Apple was content to make sharing files difficult enough to discourage casual pirates and to include the words "Don't steal music" in its iPod packaging and advertisements. Beyond that, it was up to the individual user to decide whether it's morally responsible to enjoy the work of others without paying for it.

Which brings us, of course, to this question:

Music sharing: right or wrong?
Excuse the rampant editorializing, but here are the issues surrounding music sharing as I see them. Feel free to agree or disagree, as the mood strikes you.

- Taking music that the owner would like you to pay for—
whether by copying it from an iPod, duplicating someone's audio CD, or downloading the music from the
Internet—is wrong. If you intend to keep the music, you
should pay for it. Someone (or a group of someones)
created that music with the intention of being rewarded
for their toil in ways other than your undying admiration.
If you respect the artist's work, you should also respect
the artist's desire to be paid for that work.

  Music that's intended to be shared—such as live concert
  performances, when the artists care not a whit whether you
  swap recordings with your friends—is a different matter.

- As a professional musician, I'm well aware that musicians
have been sorely abused by the recording industry. Your
mother was correct, however, when she suggested that two
wrongs don't make a right. Striking back at the recording industry by denying artists their paltry royalties is no
way to punish record executives. If you're concerned about
the rights of recording artists, visit the Recording Artists
Coalition Web site (*www.recordingartistscoalition.com*),
and lobby your elected officials to enact legislation that
protects artists' rights.

- As a consumer, I believe that it's my right to play music
I own on any compatible device I own, as long as it's
for my personal enjoyment. Currently, the law agrees.
That means that if I have one iPod, four Macs, two PCs,
one car stereo, two home stereos, a boom box, and a
portable CD player, I may make copies of that music for
each and every device I own and, if I feel so inclined,
play that same recording on every one of these devices
at the same time.

Because I believe in the rights of both musicians and con-
sumers, I will now reveal how to move the music you legally
own from your iPod to any Mac you also own. Music that
you don't own shouldn't be on your iPod in the first place;
neither should you take the music you own and dump it onto
your best friend's computer. Piracy is, indeed, a behavior issue.
So please watch your behavior.

Moving music

The iPod stores music in an invisible folder called iPod_Control. This folder is located at the root level of your iPod's hard drive. If you're a do-it-yourselfer, you can make this file and its contents visible and then drag files from the iPod to your computer's hard drive. Alternatively, a variety of utilities for the Mac and PC give you access to this invisible folder and its contents. I'll look at both the manual and assisted methods in the following sections.

The manual method (Mac OS 9)

Download a utility that's capable of turning invisible files visible. For this example, I'll use Daniel Azuma's $10 FileTyper (*www.ugcs.caltech.edu/~dazuma/filetyper*), though a host of other utilities, including Apple's ResEdit, can do the job (**Figure 4.7**).

FileTyper

Figure 4.7 FileTyper will reveal the hidden iPod_Control folder.

Then follow these steps:

1. While you're running Mac OS 9, launch FileTyper.

2. Choose Open from the File menu.

3. In the Open dialog box, navigate to the mounted iPod, and click Open.

4. Locate the iPod_Control folder, and click Select.

    Two windows will appear—one marked Folder Attribute Editor, and one marked File Attribute Editor.

5. If the Folder Attribute Editor is not active, click it.

    The entry in the first field in this window should read Device.

6. Click the Cancel button.

    Now the first field should read iPod_Control (**Figure 4.8**).

7. In this window, uncheck the check box titled Is Invisible.

8. Click the Change All button.

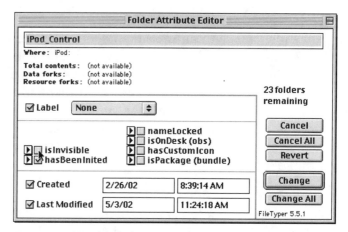

Figure 4.8 Uncheck the Is Invisible check box and click Change All to make the iPod_Control folder (and all folders within it) visible.

9. When you're asked to confirm that you really want to do this, click OK.

The Folder Attributes Editor window will disappear, leaving the File Attributes Editor window open. This window will have the word *Preferences* in the first field.

10. Click the Cancel All button.

11. Quit FileTyper.

12. Double-click the iPod's icon on the Desktop to open the iPod's hard drive.

Inside, you'll see that the iPod_Control folder is visible (**Figure 4.9**). Inside this folder are two folders: iTunes and Music. The Music folder contains all your music files inside folders that begin with the letter *F*—F0, F01, F02, and F03, for example.

Figure 4.9
The hidden revealed.

13. Use Sherlock to seek the songs you want to copy to your Mac.

14. To copy the songs, just open the appropriate folder and drag the files to your Mac's hard drive.

The manual method (Mac OS X)

The process is even simpler in Mac OS X. Here's how:

1. Mount your iPod on the Desktop.

2. Download and install a copy of Marcel Bresink's free TinkerTool (*www.bresink.de/osx/TinkerTool2.html*).

3. Choose System Preferences from the Apple menu.

4. When the System Preferences dialog opens, click TinkerTool, which appears below the Other heading.

5. In the Finder Options section of the Finder tab, check the Show Hidden and System Files check box (**Figure 4.10**).

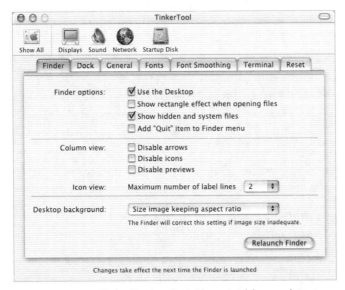

Figure 4.10 In TinkerTool, select Show Hidden and System Files and then click the Relaunch Finder button to reveal the invisible files and folders on your iPod.

6. Click the Relaunch Finder button at the bottom of the dialog.

7. Move back to the Desktop, and double-click your iPod to open its hard drive.

Inside, you'll see that the iPod_Control folder is visible.

8. Open this folder and then the Music folder within it.

Inside this folder, you'll find your music files inside folders that begin with the letter *F*—F0, F01, F02, and F03, for example (**Figure 4.11**).

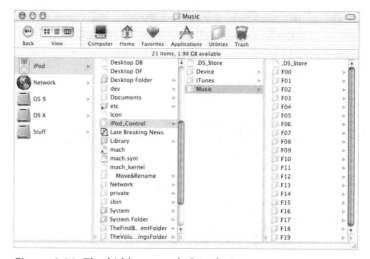

Figure 4.11 The hidden revealed (redux).

9. Use Sherlock to seek the songs you want to copy to your Mac.

10. To copy the songs, just open the appropriate folder and drag the files to your Mac's hard drive.

The manual method (Windows XP)

Revealing the iPod's hidden song files is child's play under Windows XP. Here's how:

1. Mount your iPod on your PC.

2. Open the My Computer window, and double-click the iPod.

3. Choose Folder Options from the Tools menu to open the Folder Options dialog.

4. Click the View tab.

5. Below the Hidden Files and Folders entry, click Show Hidden Files and Folders (**Figure 4.12**).

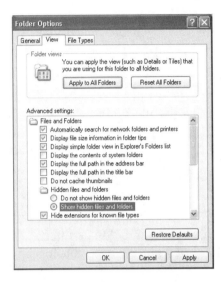

Figure 4.12
Select the Show Hidden Files and Folders option to reveal invisible items in Windows.

6. Click Apply.

The iPod_Control folder is visible.

7. Open this folder and then the Music folder within it.

Inside this folder, you'll find your music files inside folders that begin with the letter *F*—F0, F01, F02, and F03, for example (**Figure 4.13**).

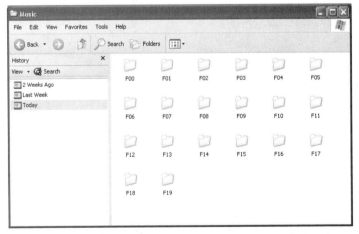

Figure 4.13 The return of the son of the hidden revealed (redux).

8. Click the Search button in the window's toolbar, and search your iPod for specific songs to copy to your PC's hard drive.

9. To copy the songs, just open the appropriate folder and drag the files to your PC's hard drive.

The assisted methods

Go to VersionTracker (*www.versiontracker.com*) and enter iPod in the Search field. You'll turn up a fair number of utilities that can assist you with moving music files from your iPod onto your computer's hard drive. Here are some of my favorites.

- **PodMaster 1000 (Mac OS 9 and Mac OS X)**
  http://homepage.mac.com/podmaster/FileSharing1.html

  The $8 PodMaster 1000 from Flying Mouse Software is an ingenious little tool that sports an iPod-like interface (**Figure 4.14**). PodMaster 1000 not only allows you to copy any number of tunes from your iPod to your Mac, but also lets you play songs from the iPod through your Mac (and its speakers). Additionally, you can view a file's ID3 tag information. Heck, it even includes a cute little Mac OS X clock that appears when you click the Apple logo in the top-left corner of the PodMaster window. PodMaster 1000 is worth every nickel of its paltry shareware fee.

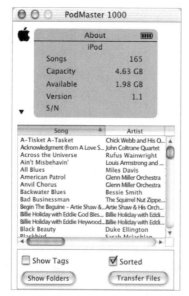

Figure 4.14
PodMaster 1000 is the most flexible of the iPod assistance utilities.

- **Podestal (Mac OS X)**
  www.codefab.com/unsupported/Podestal%20v0.1.dmg.gz

  Written by Bill Bumgarner, Podestal is a free utility that allows you to copy *any* files on your iPod to your Mac (**Figure 4.15**). The interface is divided into two tabs—one for copying music files, and the other for copying data files. Just click a file or folder, and an icon appears in the bottom-right corner of the Podestal window. (The icon represents a single item or an item-collection icon that represents more than one item.) Drag this icon to your Mac's Desktop or into an open window, and the items are copied.

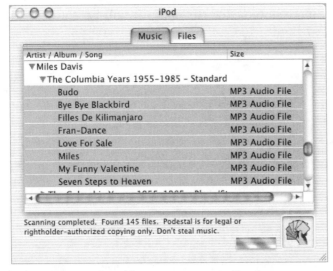

Figure 4.15 Podestal lets you copy any files from your iPod—music *and* data files.

Although you can copy the Music folder to your Mac, the files within that folder are just as invisible as they are on your iPod. Unless you want to resort to the TinkerTool trick I outlined earlier in this chapter, you'll find it easier to copy music files from Podestal's Music section.

- **OmniWeb (Mac OS X)**
www.omnigroup.com

Wait a minute—isn't OmniWeb a Web browser? Why, yes it is. But OmniWeb has a special feature that's not available in any other Mac Web browser: the capability to view the iPod's iPod_Control folder and its contents. To invoke this feature in this free-unless-you-feel-guilty-about-using-it-for-free-in-which-case-you-can-pay-$30-for-it browser, just launch OmniWeb and drag the iPod's icon to OmniWeb's main window. In a flash, all the files on your iPod are revealed in the browser (**Figure 4.16**). Double-click the iPod_Control folder to reveal the Music folder and the *F* folders within. To copy a song to your Mac, just double-click the song. It will be "downloaded" to your hard drive.

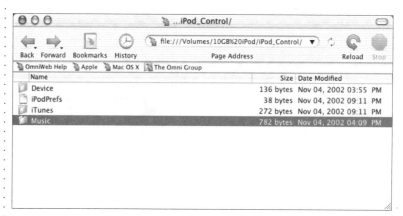

Figure 4.16 Drag and drop your iPod into OmniWeb to reveal hidden folders and files.

- **Open Pod (Mac OS X)**
http://homepage.mac.com/beweis/b_ipod.html

Open Pod is a free script that creates a new playlist within iTunes that displays all the songs on your iPod (**Figure 4.17**). From this playlist, you can copy songs from your iPod by dragging them from this playlist to your Mac's Desktop.

Figure 4.17 Select the Open iPod playlist to drag songs from your iPod to your Mac.

- **Xpod (Mac OS X)**

  http://bitcom.ch/products-xpod-e.html

  Bitcom's free Xpod is another tool with a pretty interface (**Figure 4.18**). It's less capable than PodMaster 1000 in that it doesn't allow you to select songs to copy; it's all or nothing. But it's free, it's fast, and it lets you unmount your iPod from within the application.

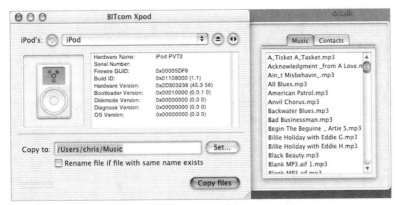

Figure 4.18 Copy all your iPod tunes to your Mac with Xpod.

■ **EphPod (Windows)**

www.ephpod.com

You heard plenty in Chapter 3 about Joe Masters' free EphPod. As I stated earlier, among its many talents is its capability to copy songs from the iPod to the Windows directory of your choosing. Just select the songs you want to copy in the Songs portion of the EphPod window, right-click one of the selected songs, and choose Copy Songs to Directory from the contextual menu (**Figure 4.19**). Navigate to the directory where you'd like to copy the songs, and click OK. The songs are copied.

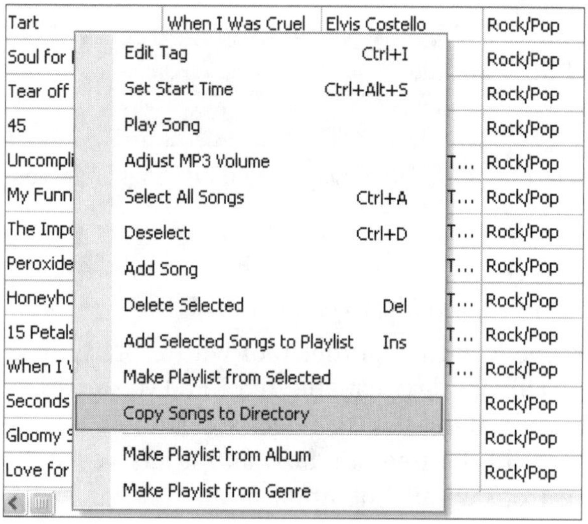

Tart	When I Was Cruel	Elvis Costello		Rock/Pop
Soul for	Edit Tag	Ctrl+I		Rock/Pop
Tear off	Set Start Time	Ctrl+Alt+S		Rock/Pop
45	Play Song			Rock/Pop
Uncompli	Adjust MP3 Volume		T...	Rock/Pop
My Funn	Select All Songs	Ctrl+A	T...	Rock/Pop
The Impc	Deselect	Ctrl+D	T...	Rock/Pop
Peroxide	Add Song		T...	Rock/Pop
Honeyho	Delete Selected	Del	T...	Rock/Pop
15 Petals	Add Selected Songs to Playlist	Ins	T...	Rock/Pop
When I \	Make Playlist from Selected		T...	Rock/Pop
Seconds	Copy Songs to Directory			Rock/Pop
Gloomy S	Make Playlist from Album			Rock/Pop
Love for	Make Playlist from Genre			Rock/Pop

Figure 4.19 EphPod allows Windows users to copy files from the iPod to the PC's hard drive.

Making
iContact

In many ways, Apple is a victim of its own success and history. How else can you explain the flood of "Is that all!?" comments that followed the initial release of the world's finest portable music player? People expect great things from Apple, and even when Apple delivers those great things—such as the first iteration of the iPod—the many-headed aren't satisfied.

Apple's first major upgrade to the iPod software—iPod Software 1.1 Update—clearly demonstrated that Apple had further plans for the iPod. If iPod users desired more from their music players, Apple was willing to provide it in the form of a simple contact manager. If those users wanted to free space in their bandolier of gadgets by leaving the Palm device at home, fine. From this day forward, the iPod will display your contacts (and more, as you'll learn in this chapter).

Getting Addressed

The iPod wasn't always a contact manager…or was it? Let's look at the history and state of the art in configuring iPod contacts.

First on the block: iPod Organizer

It would be incorrect to credit Apple with being the first to think of using the original Macintosh-compatible iPod as a personal information manager (PIM). It didn't take savvy users more than a couple of days after the iPod's general release to figure out that by creating very short, empty MP3 files and editing the Artist, Album, and Song information to include names and phone numbers, you could construct a crude contact database of your own (see the sidebar "Crude Contacts" in this section).

Only someone with few contacts or the patience of a saint would be willing to go through this kind of rigmarole. Fortunately, not long after the release of the iPod, ProVue Development (*www.provue.com*) released iPod Organizer, a $20 Macintosh application created with the company's Panorama database package.

iPod Organizer basically is a run-time version of Panorama that allows you to add information to the iPod's Song, Artist, and Album fields. It works this way:

An iPod Organizer *record* (entry) contains seven fields: Category, First Name, Last Name, Organization, Data, Source, and Notes (**Figure 5.1**). The first five fields are transferred to the iPod; the program uses the last two for internal housekeeping and for notes you want to keep on the Mac. Data entered in the Category field—something like My Friends or Burger Joints, for example—appears in the iPod's Artist screen. First Name, Last Name, and Organization appear in the Album screen. And data—phone numbers and addresses, for example—appears in the Songs screen (the information that scrolls in the iPod's display).

If you care to enter information other than phone numbers and addresses in iPod Organizer, you're welcome to do so. Create a to-do list. Jot down the few items you need to pick up at the store. Or squirrel away the computer passwords you routinely forget. Knock yourself out.

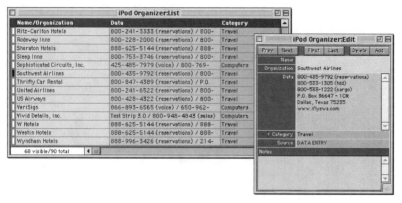

Figure 5.1 ProVue Development's iPod Organizer.

After you've entered the information you want to use in your records, iPod Organizer will move the data to iTunes. When you next update your iPod, the information you entered in iPod Organizer transfers to the iPod.

There's a lot of power and convenience on iPod Organizer's front end, thanks to the driving force of the run-time version of Panorama. But the process that takes place within iTunes and on the iPod is no different from the one I outline in the sidebar "Crude Contacts." iPod Organizer simply creates the number of empty MP3 files it needs and copies its data into the Song, Artist, and Album fields in iTunes; then iTunes transfers those MP3 files to the iPod. Very clever.

Crude Contacts

With today's iPod software you can easily create and add contacts to your Mac or Windows iPod. But if you'd care to re-create a bit of recent history and cobble together your own crude contacts, here's how:

Mac OS 9: Creating Short Audio Files with SimpleSound

1. Create and save an audio file about 5 seconds in length.

   If you're running Mac OS 9.2 or earlier, you can do this by launching SimpleSound (usually located in the Apple Extras folder inside the Mac OS 9 Applications folder) and clicking the Add button in the resulting Alert Sounds window.

   continues on next page

Crude Contacts *continued*

2. When the recording window appears, click the Record button, allow SimpleSound to record 5 seconds of silence, click Stop (if necessary), and then click the Save button (**Figure 5.2**).

Figure 5.2
Mac OS 9's SimpleSound application.

3. Give the file a descriptive name such as Blank MP3 when you're prompted.

4. Quit SimpleSound and any running applications.

5. Open the System Folder; then double-click the System file.

6. Drag your Blank MP3 file out of the System file and onto your Desktop.

Mac OS X: Creating Short Audio Files with AudioX

1. Create and save an audio file about 5 seconds in length.

   OS X doesn't include a utility for recording sound, so you'll have to grab one from the Web. AudioX (**www.realmacs.co.uk**) is a free and easy-to-use recording application.

2. Using AudioX or a similar tool, record 5 seconds of silent audio, and save your file (**Figure 5.3**).

Figure 5.3
AudioX, an easy-to-use audio recorder for Mac OS X.

3. Convert the file with iTunes.

4. Launch iTunes 2, and choose the Preferences command (in the Edit menu in Mac OS 9.2 and earlier and in the iTunes menu in Mac OS X).

5. In the iTunes Preferences dialog box, click the Importing tab, choose MP3 Encoder from the Import Using pop-up menu, and click OK (**Figure 5.4**).

6. Choose Convert to MP3 from iTunes' Advanced menu, and navigate to the Blank MP3 file you created.

iTunes will convert that file to MP3 format.

Crude Contacts *continued*

Figure 5.4
Select the MP3 Encoder in iTunes 2 to convert AIFF audio files to MP3 files.

Windows XP: Creating Short Audio Files with Sound Recorder

1. Launch Sound Recorder (located in the Entertainment folder within Windows' Accessories folder).

2. Record 5 seconds of silent audio and name and save your file.

3. Launch MusicMatch Jukebox and choose Convert from the File menu.

4. In the resulting File Format Conversion window, navigate to the folder that holds your silent file and click the folder.

5. Click the name of the file in the Highlight Files to Convert list.

6. Make sure that WAV is selected in the Source Data Type pop-up menu in the bottom-left corner of the window (**Figure 5.5**).

continues on next page

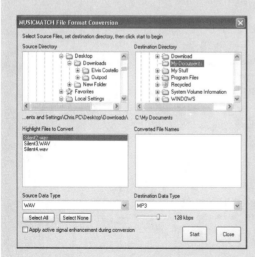

Figure 5.5
Convert a WAV file to an MP3 file in MusicMatch Jukebox.

Crude Contacts *continued*

7. In the Destination Directory list, select a destination folder for your converted file.

8. Choose MP3 from the Destination Data Type pop-up menu in the bottom-right corner of the window and click the Start button.

The file will be converted from Windows' native WAV format to MP3.

9. Open the converted MP3 file in MusicMatch Jukebox.

Adding Your Contact Information

Macintosh: To edit the tag information necessary for creating your contact, follow these steps in iTunes.

1. After you've recorded a short audio file, click the Blank MP3 "song" that's now in iTunes' main window, and press Command-I to produce the Song Information window.

2. Where the song title appears, enter your contact's name and any bit of information you'd like to scroll across the screen of your iPod—an address, for example.

3. In the Artist field, enter a bit of information that will fit on the iPod's screen—a phone number, perhaps.

4. Use the Album field for some similarly small bit of information (**Figure 5.6**).

5. Click OK.

6. Update your iPod.

7. Select your iPod in the Source list, and choose Update *the name of your iPod*.

8. Be amazed!

Figure 5.6 Rolling your own contact with iTunes 2.

Crude Contacts *continued*

Windows: The steps for editing tags in MusicMatch Jukebox are remarkably similar to the iTunes procedure.

1. In MusicMatch Jukebox, right-click the silent file and choose Edit Track Tags from the contextual menu.

2. Where the song title appears, enter your contact's name and any bit of information you'd like to scroll across the screen of your iPod—an address, for example.

3. In the Artist field, enter a bit of information that will fit on the iPod's screen—a phone number, perhaps.

4. Use the Album field for some similarly small bit of information.

5. Click Apply; then click OK.

6. Drag the silent file from the main Playlist window to your iPod in the Portable Devices window.

Detach your iPod from your computer, navigate to the Songs screen, scroll down until you find the contact you just created, and click the Select button. The information you entered in the Song Title field will scroll across the screen from right to left, and the Artist and Album information will appear below. If the information advances too quickly to the next song (after all, the iPod thinks that it's a 5-second song and will go on to the next tune after it's finished playing your short ditty), click the Play/Pause button to pause playback.

To refine this technique but lose one of your fields, create several of these files, and enter the same information in the Album or Artist field—My Family, for example. This method allows you to group contacts.

You can also group contacts by creating group playlists—playlists that contain nothing but the names of members of your family or the members of your company softball team.

Last step: Breathe a sigh of relief that you no longer have to do this kind of thing to get contacts into your iPod.

Viva vCard

Whether iPod Organizer motivated Apple to add its own contact management to the iPod is something that only Apple knows. All that really matters is that Apple was motivated thusly, and contacts became part of the iPod experience with the release of iPod Software 1.1 Update (and remained a part of that experience in subsequent software updates).

The magic behind contact management on the iPod is the vCard standard.

The vCard standard

In the mid-1990s, Apple, AT&T, IBM, and Siemens founded an initiative called Versit that created the *vCard* standard. This standard allows you to store electronically such information as names, addresses (business, home, mailing, and parcel), telephone numbers (home, business, fax, pager, mobile, ISDN, voice, data, and video), email addresses, and Internet addresses on computers, personal information managers, and cellular telephones. The standard also offers graphics support for photographs and logos. Audio and time-zone information is supported as well. The standard is platform-agnostic so you can share vCards among computers running a variety of operating systems—Mac OS, Windows, and Linux, for example—as well as with cellular phones and personal digital assistants, such as devices running the Palm operating system. vCard support is built into products from such vendors as Apple, IBM, Lotus, Lucent Technologies, Netscape, Power On Software, and Microsoft.

vCard and you

Fascinating as the history of the vCard format may be, its story becomes a lot more gripping when you understand that with very little muss or fuss, you can move information from products that support versions 2.1 and 3.0 of the vCard standard to your iPod. Before you break out the champagne, however, you should know that the iPod supports only a portion of the vCard standard. You can't view a graphic, for example, or listen to a sound contained in a vCard file stored on your iPod.

Here's the information that your iPod *can* display:

- **Contact's formatted name** (Bubba Jones, for example).
- **Contact's name.** The name as it appears in the contact (Jones, Bubba, Dr., for example).
- **Contact's address(es).** The address types supported by vCard (business, home, mailing, and parcel).
- **Contact's telephone number(s).** The phone numbers supported by vCard.
- **Contact's email.** The email addresses in the contact.
- **Contact's title.** Dr., Ms., Mr., and so on.

- **Contact's organization.** The company name displayed in the contact.
- **Contact's URL.** The Internet address contained in the contact.
- **Contact's note.** The note field in the contact.

vCard support wouldn't mean much if common applications didn't support it. Fortunately, the universal nature of the standard means that vCard is supported by most information-management and email applications you're likely to run across. As this book goes to press, vCard support is present on the Mac in OS X's Address Book, Qualcomm's Eudora and Microsoft's Entourage email clients, and Palm's Palm Desktop 4.0 and Power On Software's Now Contact information managers. And for Windows, you'll find vCard supported in such mainstays as Windows' Address Book, Microsoft Outlook, and Palm Desktop. (The Windows version of Qualcomm's Eudora doesn't support vCards.)

---

iPod Sorting

Before the release of the iPod Software 1.2 Updater, you were limited in how you could sort contacts on the iPod. If a contact's name within the vCard began with his or her first name, by gum, that's how it would be displayed on the iPod. Sure, you could edit the vCard file to swap the position of each contact's first and last name, but what an unholy bother.

Fortunately, Apple has made contact sorting much easier. Just highlight the Settings entry in the iPod's main screen, press Select, and scroll down to Contacts. Press Select again and you'll find the Sort and Display options. Each option allows you to select First and Last or Last and First, thus allowing you to sort by last name, but display your contacts' first name first and last name...well, last.

Working with Contacts

Now that you understand the underlying structure of the iPod's contacts, you're ready to put them to practical use. In the following pages, you'll create contacts in various applications and export them to the iPod. Along the way, I'll show you ways to move unexpected information to your iPod.

The manual method: Macintosh

Much like their paper counterparts, vCards are amenable to being dropped where they can be most helpful. In the case of vCards, this means that they can be dragged from their host application (Mac OS X's Address Book application or Microsoft Entourage 2001 running under Mac OS 9, for example) onto your Mac's Desktop or into another vCard-friendly application.

Wouldn't it be swell if they could just as easily be dropped into your iPod?

They can. Here's how:

Step 1: Locating contacts in host applications

To find vCard-compatible contact information in the following programs, follow these instructions.

Address Book (Mac OS X)

1. Open Address Book.

    You'll find it in Mac OS X's Application's folder at the root level of your startup drive. All the contacts appear in the main window.

2. To select all the contacts, press Command-A; to select individual contacts, Command-click each contact you want to select.

Microsoft Entourage 2001 (for Mac OS 9.2 and earlier and OS X's Classic environment)

1. Open Entourage 2001 (inside the Microsoft Office folder).

2. In the Folder List field click the Address Book entry, choose Address Book from the Window menu, or press Command-2 to display your contacts in the main Entourage window.

3. Click a contact; then press Command-A to select all the contacts, or Command-click to select numerous individual contacts.

Microsoft Entourage X (Mac OS X)

1. Open Entourage X (inside the Microsoft Office folder).

2. Click the Address Book button in the top-left portion of the main window, choose Address Book from the

View menu's Go To submenu, or press Command-2 to produce the Address Book.

3. Click a contact; then press Command-A to select all the contacts, or Command-click to select numerous individual contacts.

Palm Desktop 4.x for Macintosh

1. Open Palm Desktop.

2. If the Address List window isn't visible, choose Address List from the Window menu.

3. Click a contact and press Command-A to select all the contacts, or Command-click to select numerous individual contacts.

Versions of Palm Desktop before version 4.x do not support the vCard standard.

Eudora 5.1 and Now Contact 4.x for Macintosh

Although the current versions of Eudora and Now Contact support the vCard standard, dragging contacts from these applications' address books onto the Desktop does not create vCard files. Later in this chapter, I'll show you some utilities you can use to extract vCard contacts from Eudora and Now Contact.

Step 2: Moving contacts into the iPod manually

Now that you've located the contacts you want to move, you can move them. Follow these steps:

1. If your iPod's not connected to your Mac, make the connection, and wait for its icon to appear on the Desktop.

2. Configure your iPod so that it mounts on the Mac's Desktop as an external hard drive.

   To do this in iTunes 2, open the iPod Preferences dialog box, and check the Enable FireWire Disk Use checkbox (**Figure 5.7**).

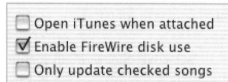

Figure 5.7
Choose Enable FireWire Disk Use to mount your iPod on the Desktop.

3. Double-click the iPod icon on the Desktop to open the iPod's hard drive.

4. Locate and open the Contacts folder on this hard drive (**Figure 5.8**).

Figure 5.8
The iPod's Calendars and Contacts folders.

5. Open the application that holds the vCards you want to add to your iPod.

6. Select the vCards in that application, and drag them into the Contacts folder.

7. Disconnect your iPod by dragging its icon to the Trash.

8. Wait for the iPod to reboot, and navigate to the Contacts screen.

The contacts you copied are displayed in the Contacts list.

The manual method: Windows

Moving contacts manually from Windows applications to the iPod isn't terribly different from performing the operation on the Mac. Here's how to go about it:

Step 1: Locating contacts in host applications

To find vCard-compatible contact information in the following programs, follow these instructions.

Address Book (Microsoft Windows)

1. Launch Address Book.

2. If it's not already selected, choose Main Identity's Contacts in the Address Book window's left pane.

3. Press Control-A to select all the contacts, hold the Control key while clicking on non-contiguous contacts to select multiple contacts individually, or hold down the Shift key while clicking on two contacts (those two contacts and all contacts between them will be selected).

Microsoft Outlook (Windows)

1. Open Microsoft Outlook.

2. Click the Contacts button in the Outlook Shortcuts portion of the Microsoft Outlook window.

3. Press Control-A to select all the contacts, hold the Control key while clicking noncontiguous contacts to select multiple contacts individually, or hold down the Shift key while clicking two contacts—those two contacts and all contacts between them will be selected.

Palm Desktop 4.x for Windows

1. Open Palm Desktop.

2. If the Address List window isn't visible, click the Address button in the left portion of the Palm Desktop window.

3. Press Control-A to select all the contacts, hold down the Control key while clicking noncontiguous contacts to select multiple contacts individually, or hold down the Shift key while clicking two contacts (those two contacts and all contacts between them will be selected).

Step 2: Moving contacts into the iPod manually

Regrettably, not all the Windows applications I mention support drag and drop. But there's more than one way to skin a contact. To move contacts from each of these applications, follow these steps.

Address Book and Microsoft Outlook (Microsoft Windows)

1. Open the Contacts folder inside your iPod.

    You'll find your iPod by double-clicking My Computer.

2. Switch to Address Book or Outlook and drag and drop your contacts into the iPod's Contacts folder. Your contacts have been moved to the iPod as individual vCard files.

3. Unmount your iPod by clicking the iPod icon in the Notification area (once known as the System Tray) and choosing Unmount from the resulting contextual menu.

4. When the iPod displays the message "OK to disconnect," detach the FireWire cable.

5. Wait for the iPod to reboot; then navigate to the Contacts screen.

    The contacts you copied are displayed in the Contacts list.

Palm Desktop 4.x for Windows

1. With your contacts selected in Palm Desktop, choose Export vCard from Palm Desktop's File menu.

2. In the resulting Export As window, navigate to your iPod's Contacts folder.

3. Making sure that vCard File (*vcf) is displayed in the Export type field, enter a name for your contact file in the File Name field and click the Export button.

    Your contacts will be moved to the iPod as a single vCard file.

4. Unmount your iPod by clicking the iPod icon in the Notification area and choosing Unmount from the resulting contextual menu.

5. When the iPod displays the message "OK to disconnect," detach the FireWire cable.

6. Wait for the iPod to reboot; then navigate to the Contacts screen.

    The contacts you copied will be displayed in the Contacts list.

You've probably heard (and if not, you'll soon learn) that many utilities for automating this process are available. If so, why use the manual method? To begin with, as this book goes to press, such utilities for Windows are fairly rare and those that exist work only with Microsoft's Outlook. And many of the Mac utilities work only with Mac OS X. If you run Mac OS 9.2 or earlier or don't use Outlook but want to move your contacts from a particular application, moving vCard manually may be your only choice. Also, I can't anticipate future applications that will offer vCard support or whether these applications will offer an expedient way to move contact information between your computer and the iPod. As long as the host application supports exporting contacts as vCards, the manual method should see you through until something more convenient comes along.

Multiple Contacts in a Single File

If you drag multiple vCards into the iPod's Contact folder, that folder will be jammed with files. If you're keen on both tidiness and repetitive tasks, you can place your contacts in a single .vcf file. To do so, just select a .vcf file as a master file and open it in a text editor. Then open each .vcf file in the Contacts folder in that same text editor, and cut and paste the information in the file into the master file.

Your master file will look something like this:

```
begin:vcard
fn:Costello\, Elvis
n:Costello;Elvis;;;
email;type=internet:thebestelvis@mcmanus.com
end:vcard
begin:vcard
fn:Blow\, Joe
n:Blow;Joe;;;
tel;type=work:555/555-1212
email;type=internet:joe@blow.com
org:Joe Blow Inc
end:vcard
begin:vcard
fn:Jones\, Bubba
n:Jones;Bubba;;Dr.;
adr;type=work:111 Main Street;Anytown;AK;99988;USA
adr;type=home:543 Home Street;Anytown;AK;99988;
tel;type=home:555/555-1213
tel;type=work:555/555-1212
tel;type=cell:555/555-1234
email;type=internet:bubba@bubba.com
org:Bub Industries
url;type=home:www.bubba.com
note:Bubba loves chocolate cake!
end:vcard
```

The automated method: Macintosh

Now that you've learned to crawl through iPod contact management when you need to, it's time to spread your wings and fly. The following automation methods will make working with contacts on your Mac much easier.

iSync

Before the release of the iPod Software 1.2 Updater, Apple provided AppleScripts for automating the transfer of contacts between Mac OS X's Address Book, Microsoft's Entourage, and Palm's Palm Desktop and the iPod. Apple has since removed those AppleScripts from its site.

Why? Because Apple believes it has a better solution—a utility called iSync.

iSync, as the name implies, synchronizes contact and calendar data between the Mac and such devices as the iPod, Palm computing devices, compatible cell phones, and—if you have a .Mac account (Apple's online service)—other Macs. Regrettably, iSync works only with the data stored in Mac OS X's Address Book and Apple's calendar application, iCal. (Dry those tears, Entourage and Palm Desktop users; see the sidebar "I Need Contact!" to learn how to move your contacts into Address Book.)

iSync requires that you be running Mac OS X 10.2 (Jaguar) or later. To sync your iPod with Address Book, follow these steps.

1. Download a copy of iSync from *www.apple.com/isync*.

2. Launch iSync, and choose Add Device from the Devices menu.

    Your iPod should appear in the resulting Add Devices window.

3. Double-click the iPod's icon and it will be added to iSync's window.

    The iSync window will expand to reveal the synchronization options (**Figure 5.9**).

Figure 5.9
Synchronization options within Apple's iSync.

In the iSync window, you can switch on synchronization with the iPod as well as choose whether you want to synchronize your iPod automatically when it's connected. You can also enable contact and calendar synchronization by checking the Contacts and Calendars check boxes (which are checked by default). Within the Calendars portion of the window, you can choose to synchronize all calendars or select individual calendars (your work and home calendars, but not your child's soccer schedule calendar, for example).

4. To synchronize your contact and calendar data between the iPod and Address Book and iCal, click the Sync Now button in the iSync window.

   The synchronization process begins. Before iSync moves any data to the iPod, it issues a warning via the Safeguard window (**Figure 5.10**). If you've enabled synchronization between both Address Book and iCal, the first Safeguard window indicates how many contacts will be added to your iPod, how many will be removed, and how many will be modified.

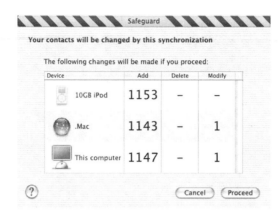

Figure 5.10
iSync's not-so-subtle Safeguard window.

5. To finish synchronizing your contacts, click the Proceed button in the Safeguard window; to cancel the operation, click Cancel.

A different Safeguard window appears if you've also enabled calendar synchronization. Here iSync tells you how many calendar and To Do items will be added, removed, and modified. Again, click Proceed to synchronize your data.

Note: Don't be alarmed if you see a message indicating that the synchronization has failed. If more than one device appears in the iSync window—such as your iPod and Palm Computing device—and not all devices are present and accounted for (you haven't plugged in your Palm cradle, for example), iSync will synchronize the devices it can find and then report a failure for those devices it can't find.

I Need Contact!

If, like many Mac users, you've carefully squirreled away your contacts in Microsoft's Entourage or Palm's Palm Desktop, you may be disappointed that iSync works only with Address Book. But, as Aristotle was so fond of saying, "It's no use crying over spilled goat's milk."

If you want to use iSync, you must use Address Book. Fortunately, it's not difficult to move contacts from either program into Address Book. Here's how:

continues on next page

I Need Contact! *continued*

Entourage

1. Create an empty folder on your Mac's Desktop, and give it an intuitive name, such as Entourage Contacts.

2. Launch Entourage, and click the Address Book button.

3. Select the contacts you'd like to move to OS X's Address Book from Entourage's Address Book window.

4. Click the highlighted addresses, and drag them from the Address Book window into the Entourage Contacts folder you created.

   The contacts will be copied to the folder as individual vCards.

5. Launch OS X's Address Book, and drag the Entourage Contacts folder into either the Group or Name portion of the window.

   In a flash, your contacts will appear in Address Book, ready for exporting to your iPod via iSync.

   Note: This trick works exactly the same way with the Mac OS 9 version of Entourage in Mac OS X's Classic environment.

Palm Desktop (version 4.0 and later)

1. Launch Palm Desktop, and choose Address List from the Window menu.

2. Select the contacts you'd like to move to OS X's Address Book in Palm Desktop's Address List window.

3. Choose Export from the File menu.

4. In the resulting Export: Palm Desktop window, name your file, select the Desktop as the destination for your saved file, and choose vCard from the Format pop-up menu.

5. Click the Export button.

   A vCard containing all the selected contacts will be saved to the Desktop.

6. Open Address Book, and drag the vCard into either the Group or Name portion of the window. In a flash, your contacts appear in Address Book ready for exporting to your iPod via iSync.

Older Contact Managers

Those who use older contact managers, such as TouchBase and DynoDex, may believe that they've been left out of the party. Not so. Although these contact managers won't run in Mac OS X (or, likely, in Mac OS 9), you can still pull their data into Address Book. The means for doing so is Palm Desktop.

Palm Desktop began life as Claris Organizer and it has retained the file compatibility it had in its Claris incarnation. Just use Palm Desktop's Import command to open your old contact-manager file (you may need to move a few fields around during the import process to make the data line up correctly) and then export it as a vCard file.

Eudora 5.1 (Mac OS 9 and OS X)

Although the Macintosh version of Qualcomm's Eudora 5.1 supports the vCard standard, contacts in the program's Address Book are not saved in the vCard format. To move your Eudora addresses to the iPod, therefore, you must convert them.

To do so, download Andreas Amann's free Eudora vCard Export utility from *http://homepage.mac.com/aamann/EudoravCard-Export.sit*. Then, to use the program, follow these steps:

1. Launch Eudora vCard Export, and choose the sort order you prefer from the Sort Order pop-up menu (first name, last name or last name, first name) (**Figure 5.11**).

Figure 5.11
Eudora's vCard
Export preferences.

2. Locate your Eudora folder (inside the Documents folder, which is inside your Mac OS X Users folder), and drag it on top of the Eudora vCard Export icon.

   When the program is finished converting Eudora's contacts, it will create a Contacts folder on the Mac's Desktop and place the converted .vcf files in that folder.

3. Drag the .vcf files into the Contacts folder inside the iPod.

   Your iPod must be mounted on the Desktop for you to do this.

   The Eudora vCard Export utility can't pull contact information from mailing-list entries that contain groups of contacts. The program can handle only individual contacts.

Now Contact (Mac OS X and OS 9)

Two tools are available for moving contacts out of version 4.x of Power On Software's Now Contact personal information manager application. The first is NowPak for iPod (*http://poweronsoftware.com/products/nudc/contact2ipd.asp*), a free, OS X-only AppleScript produced by Now Software that transfers both contact and calendar information from Now's Now Contact and Now Up-to-Date. The other is NETsettings NowPod (*www.netsettings.com*), a free utility that works with both Mac OS 9 and Mac OS X. The two utilities work in slightly different ways. Here's how to export your contacts with each utility.

NowPak for iPod (Mac OS X only)

1. Make sure that the iPod is mounted on the Desktop.

2. Launch Now Contact.

3. Launch Now Contact to iPod.

4. When you're prompted, pick an iPod to update (and if you have more than one on your Desktop, aren't you the lucky duck?); then click Select.

5. If you've already run this script once, you'll see a warning that an entry already exists for this address book.

   You can cancel the process, append contacts that you've added since you last ran the script, or overwrite the preceding entry.

6. When you're given the option to display names by last name first or first name first, make your selection and then click Select.

   The script will do its work and inform you of its success when the job is done.

7. Click Done to complete the process and quit the script.

8. Drag the iPod to the Trash to unmount it.

   When the iPod reboots, you'll find your contacts in the list of contacts in the iPod's Contacts screen.

NETsettings NowPod (Mac OS 9 and OS X)

1. Make sure that the iPod is mounted on the Desktop.

2. Launch Now Contact.

3. Launch NETsettings NowPod.

4. Choose Preferences from the Edit menu to open the Preferences dialog box.

5. Click the General Preferences tab (**Figure 5.12**), and choose the Reverse Names option to have the iPod display names in reverse order from the way that they're displayed in Now Contact (last name first, for example).

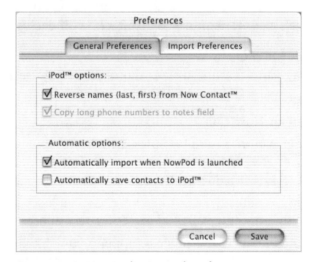

Figure 5.12 NowPod's General preferences.

6. Choose the Automatically Import When NowPod Is Launched option if that sounds like a good idea or the Automatically Save Contacts to iPod option if you prefer not to copy contacts to the iPod manually.

7. Click the Import Preferences tab (**Figure 5.13**), and select the information you'd like to import to your iPod.

Options include work address, home address, email address, work phone, home phone, mobile phone, and fax phone.

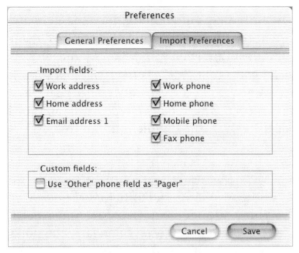

Figure 5.13 NowPod's Import preferences.

8. Check the Use "Other" Phone Field As "Pager" checkbox if this option appeals to you.

9. Click Save to save your choices.

10. Switch to Now Contact, and display only those contacts that you want to import to the iPod.

Select all the contacts that begin with the letter B, for example, and choose Find Selected from the Find menu to display just those contacts. NowPod will import only the contacts that are displayed.

11. Switch back to NowPod, and click Import.

Unless you've configured NowPod to place your contacts on the iPod automatically, you'll be prompted for a location in which to save the exported .vcf file.

12. If you've chosen to move your contacts to the iPod manually, drag the .vcf file you just created to the iPod's Contacts folder.

The automated method: Windows

As this book goes to press, it's still early days for the Windows iPod. For that reason, only a few utilities are available for moving your contacts to your iPod. Those utilities that do exist, work solely with Microsoft Outlook, the email client and personal information manager included with Microsoft Office. Of those utilities I'm keen on Mike Matheson's iPodSync (*http://iccnet.50megs.com/Products/iPodSync/index.htm*), Conrad Hagenmans' iAppoint (*www.hagemans.com/iPod*), Oliver Stoer's Outpod (*www.stoer.de/downloads/Outpod.zip*), and Joe Masters' EphPod (*www.ephpod.com*), which are all free.

iPodSync

iPodSync is Mike Matheson's attempt to recreate the Mac's iSync application on Windows. For the most part, he succeeds quite well. Within the iPodSync window you can choose to synchronize your Outlook contacts, calendars, and notes to your iPod. To move your contacts to the iPod, follow these steps:

1. Mount your iPod as a FireWire disk on your PC.

2. Launch iPodSync and click the Contacts button.

3. In the expanded window that appears, select the Synchronize Contacts option (**Figure 5.14**).

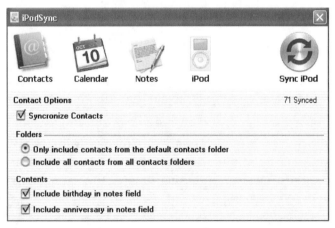

Figure 5.14 iPodSync's contact synchronization options.

4. Select the option "Only Include Contacts from the Default Contacts Folder" or the option "Include All Contacts from All Contacts Folders."

5. In the Contents portion of the window, choose whether to include birthday and anniversary events in the Notes field.

6. Click the Sync iPod button to copy your contacts to the iPod.

   Your Outlook contacts will be copied as a single vCard file (called contacts) to your iPod's Contacts folder.

iAppoint

iAppoint can also move both Outlook calendar and contact information to the iPod. To use it for this purpose, follow along.

1. Mount your iPod as a FireWire disk on your PC.

2. Launch iAppoint and click the Contacts button.

3. In the resulting window, enter a path to your iPod's Contacts folder in the Save path field—e:\Contacts\ contacts.vcf, for example—if your iPod appears as the E drive on your PC (**Figure 5.15**).

Figure 5.15 Enter the path to your iPod in iAppoint.

4. Disable the options to save birthday and anniversary data to each contact if you don't want that information displayed on your iPod.

5. Click the Start button to copy your Outlook contacts to the iPod.

Your contacts will be copied as a single vCard file (called contacts) to your iPod's Contacts folder.

Note that unlike iPodSync, iAppoint will copy only your default contacts to your iPod.

OutPod

Yes, OutPod can transfer calendar and contact information, too. Here's how:

1. Mount your iPod as a FireWire disk on your PC.

2. Launch OutPod, and click the Contacts entry in the left side of the OutPod window.

Your Outlook contacts will appear in the right side of the window (**Figure 5.16**).

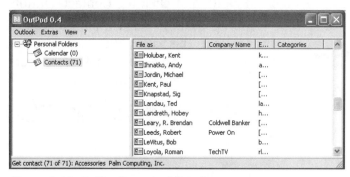

Figure 5.16 OutPod's contact-list view.

3. Select those contacts that you want to copy to your iPod.

4. From the Outlook menu choose Save Selected Items if you want to save each contact as a separate vCard file, or choose Save Selected Items in One File if you want to save your contacts in a single file.

5. If you choose the first command, you'll be presented with the Browse for Folder window. In this window, navigate to your iPod's Contacts folder and click OK to copy your contacts to the iPod.

6. If you choose the second command, a Save As dialog box appears. In this dialog box, name the contact file, navigate to the iPod's Contacts folder, and click Save to copy your contacts to the iPod.

Windows may toss up a warning that an outside application is attempting to access data from Outlook. That warning is for your protection. Some viruses, for example, may attempt to grab Outlook contact information in this same way. To allow OutPod to do its job, click the Allow Access For option and choose 1 minute from the pop-up menu. These settings give OutPod plenty of time to transfer your contacts before shutting the door on this kind of activity.

EphPod

Among its many talents, EphPod can display your Outlook contacts and synchronize them on the iPod while it's also synchronizing the iPod's music library. Additionally, you can create new contacts from within EphPod. Here's how to do it all:

1. Mount your iPod as a FireWire disk on your PC.

2. Launch EphPod and click Get Outlook Contacts in the toolbar.

3. You'll see an alert that Outlook may toss up the warning I mentioned earlier. Click Yes to proceed.

4. In the Microsoft Outlook warning dialog box that appears, click the Allow Access For option, choose 1 minute from the pop-up menu, and click Yes.

5. When the hourglass icon disappears, click the Contacts entry in the iPod View portion of the EphPod window.

   Your contacts will appear in a column to the right of the Column entry (**Figure 5.17**).

Figure 5.17
Contacts displayed
in EphPod.

6. Click the Sync Folders button in the toolbar.

Your contacts will be transferred to your iPod.

EphPod has a couple of other contacts-related tricks up its sleeve. If you double-click a contact, for example, you can edit the information in it. This trick is useful if you want to add a note at the last minute before moving your contacts to the iPod.

You can also create a new contact by choosing New Contact from the File menu. You'll be asked to enter a name for your contact; then the Contact Information window appears. In that window, you can enter such information as your contact's email address, phone number, and work and home addresses (**Figure 5.18**).

Figure 5.18
You can edit and create contacts within EphPod.

In addition, you can create memos and move those memos to your iPod. One way to do this is to choose New Memo (As Contact) from the File menu and then enter text in the resulting Edit Memo window. Or you can choose Import Memo from File to create a memo from an existing text file. After the transfer, both types of memos will appear as contacts on your iPod.

Removing contacts from your iPod

So you've broken up with your boyfriend, your favorite dry cleaner has gone out of business, or you can't recall who this "Jane" person is? There's no need to pack your iPod with contacts you don't need; you can remove them easily. Here's how:

1. If your iPod's not connected to your computer, make the connection, and wait for its icon to appear on the Mac's Desktop or Windows' My Computer window.

2. Configure your iPod so that it mounts on the computer as an external hard drive.

3. Double-click the iPod icon to open the iPod's hard drive.

4. Locate and open the Contacts folder on this hard drive.

5. Select the contacts you'd like to remove, and drag them to the Trash on the Mac or the Recycle Bin on the PC.

6. Disconnect your iPod by dragging its icon to the Trash on the Mac or by unmounting it in Windows Navigation area (a.k.a. the System Tray).

   If the contact you want to remove is part of a single vCard file that contains multiple names, you can edit the contact out in a text editor. Just open the vCard file in a text editor, delete the BEGIN:vCard and END:vCard entries (and everything in between), and the contact will be gone (see "Hacking a .vcf file" later in this chapter for more information).

Beyond Addresses

Sure, Apple made its intentions pretty clear when it added the Contacts heading to the iPod's main screen, but there's no reason on earth why you have to use the Contacts area as a location for storing names and addresses. Think outside the stainless-steel-and-Lucite box, and you can come up with countless ways to move the information you need to your iPod.

For instance? Well, how about:

- Notes for your important business meeting
- Your grocery list
- Favorite recipes
- Your master birding list
- Your to-do list for that day
- Car-rental and hotel reservation confirmation numbers
- For your next overseas vacation, translations of the phrases "Where can I exchange money?", "Where is the bathroom, please?", and "No, honestly, I'm Canadian; please stop sneering at me."

In short, any information that you keep on a small piece of paper and jam into your pocket or purse, you can easily store on your iPod.

Placing the information on your iPod is a simple matter. You can do so by editing an existing .vcf file or by using a contact manager or Address Book program. The following section shows you how to create a file that contains the Spanish translation for the phrase "Meatballs, didn't I tell you?" into Spanish via both methods.

Hacking a .vcf file

To edit an existing .vcf file, follow these steps:

1. With your iPod mounted, make a copy of a .vcf file, and open that file in a text editor such as Mac OS X's TextEdit, Mac OS 9's SimpleText, or Windows' Notepad.

   You'll see something like this:

   ```
   BEGIN:vCard
   VERSION:2.1
   FN:Elvis Costello
   N:Costello;Elvis
   EMAIL;INTERNET:thebestelvis@mcmanus.com
   END:vCard
   ```

2. Delete EMAIL;INTERNET:thebestelvis@mcmanus.com.

3. Remove the words following FN: and N:, and enter the word Meatballs.

   Note: There are no spaces between the colon and the first word.

4. In the line after N:Meatballs, enter NOTE:.

5. Following NOTE:, enter ¿Albóndigas, no te dije?.

6. Save the file, and copy it to your iPod's Contact folder.

7. Unmount your iPod.

8. When the iPod reboots, choose Contacts from the main menu; scroll down to the Meatballs entry; and burst into happy tears, knowing that you'll never be at a loss for words when you spy meatballs in a Spanish-speaking country.

To add a carriage return so that a space appears between lines, enter \n at the end of the line. For your text to appear in this form:

```
Hola Isabel,
¿Cómo estás?
¿Albóndigas, no te dije?
Cristobal
```

You'd type:

```
Hola Isabel,\n¿Cómo estás?\n¿Albóndigas, no te dije?
\nCristobal
```

Entering data via an email client or contact manager

If the manual method is more than you can bear, do the job with a program such as Palm Desktop, Microsoft Entourage or Outlook, or Mac OS X or Windows' own Address Book. Follow these steps:

1. With your iPod mounted, launch one of the applications listed in the preceding section.

2. Create a new contact.

3. In the First Name field, enter Meatballs.

4. In the Title field, enter ¿Albóndigas, no te dije?.

5. Close and, if necessary, save the contact (**Figure 5.19**).

Figure 5.19 Roll your own vCard with Mac OS X's Address Book.

6. Drag the Meatballs contact from the application to the Mac or PC's Desktop (**Figure 5.20**).

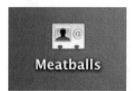

Figure 5.20
The results of your handiwork.

7. Drag the resulting Meatballs.vcf file into your iPod's Contacts folder.

8. Unmount your iPod.

9. When the iPod reboots, choose Contacts from the Extras menu; scroll down to the Meatballs entry; and do a little dance, knowing that this helpful phrase is just a couple of clicks away.

Why use the Title field rather than a Note field? Your email client or contact manager may not offer a field for notes. Truth be told, it doesn't really matter what kind of field you use. The vCard standard will allow you to enter text in any supported field. The Title field has several advantages: It's used in all email clients and contact managers, it's rarely used in the applications, and it's supported by the iPod.

Additional utilities of interest

After Apple opened the door to accessing information on the iPod, it didn't take developers and hobbyists long to find ways to exploit that capability. Up to this point, most efforts had been directed toward moving the information intended for the iPod—names, addresses, and phone numbers—to the device. But some intrepid individuals have strayed from this obvious goal and devised some unexpected uses for the iPod's contact capabilities.

iPodIt (Mac OS X only)

www.ipod-it.com

Michael Zapp's $15 iPodIt can move a wealth of information to your iPod—including your Microsoft Entourage mail, calendars, notes, and to-do tasks as well as driving directions and weather forecasts (**Figure 5.21**). iPodIt is comprised of an application and AppleScript. You can also delete groups of items—weather forecasts, events, and mail, for example—from within the program. iPodIt supercedes Zapp's previous iPod applications EntourageEvents, EntourageMail, and EntourageNotes.

Figure 5.21
iPodIt's many synchronization options.

PodNews (Mac OS X only)

www.clichesw.com/podnews

Cliché Software's free PodNews uploads notes you create, weather information, song lyrics and news headlines—and some full stories—from more than 300 news sites (including

MacCentral, iPoding.com, and Slashdot) to your iPod (**Figure 5.22**). Items appear in the Contact section of the iPod. Those stories that exceed the iPod's limit of 1,000 characters per page are broken into multiple stories. Future plans include the option to download driving directions and stock quotes.

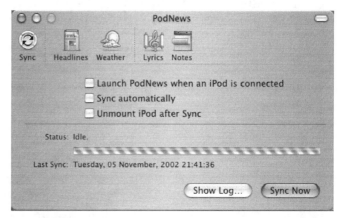

Figure 5.22 PodNews places headlines and news stories on your iPod.

iPodMemo (Mac OS X and OS 9)

www.versiontracker.com

Yup, another text editor, but it's the rare one that works with Mac OS 9 as well as Mac OS X. This free utility from Sebastien Jeanquier has a simple interface that contains an area for entering the subject of your note and another, larger field for the message body (**Figure 5.23**).

iPodMemo sports two particularly attractive features. The first is a small counter in the top-right corner of the program's window that indicates how many characters you've written. (Notes are limited to 1,000 characters.) The second is a Control menu that contains three useful commands: a command to sync a note to a mounted iPod, another command to unmount a mounted iPod, and a third command to open the mounted iPod's Contacts folder.

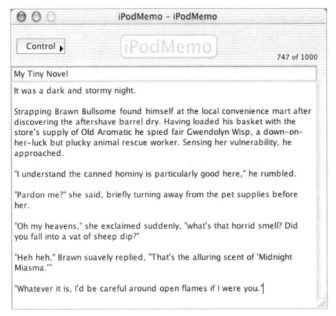

Figure 5.23 Take your novel-in-progress with you with iPodMemo.

Pod2Go (Mac OS X only)

www.kainjow.com/pod2go/website

Kevin Wojniak's free Pod2Go is another utility for downloading headlines and weather (**Figure 5.24**). Similar to PodNews (though missing the song lyrics and memo features), Pod2Go can auto-sync when you plug in your iPod.

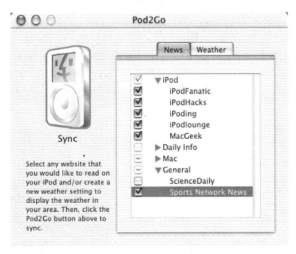

Figure 5.24 You want that Pod2Go?

PodWriter (Mac OS X only)

http://steigerworld.com/doug/podwriter.php

The name pretty well describes the function. PodWriter is Doug Steigerwald's free Cocoa application for creating notes that you then copy to your iPod (**Figure 5.25**). Just enter a title, description, and text; save the note; and drop it into your iPod's Contacts folder. The note takes up residence on the iPod. You can also import text into PodWriter. The latest version allows you to spell-check your notes with Mac OS X's built-in spell checker.

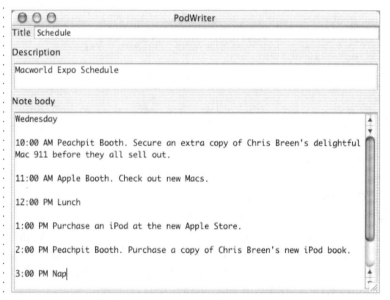

Figure 5.25 PodWriter is another handy iPod note-taker.

To seek out additional contact utilities, drop by VersionTracker (*www.versiontracker.com*) and enter iPod in the search field in the Macintosh and Windows sections. In next to no time, VersionTracker will present a rich list of utilities for your portable pal.

Make a Date

6

After Apple sanctioned the iPod for use as a contact keeper, none of us should have slapped our foreheads and bellowed, *"Who woulda thunk it!?"* when the diminutive device was later updated to display calendars. Contact and calendar management go hand in hand, and if the iPod was going to serve as a personal information manager, eventually it also had to support calendars.

With version 1.2 of the iPod software, it does on both the Mac and Windows iPod models.

Such support likely wouldn't exist were it not for standards that make it easy to move calendar information from one place to another—computer to computer, computer to the Web, and computer to iPod, for example. Fortunately, such standards live in the form of vCalendar and iCalendar—universal formats similar to the vCard standard that allow you to transport contact information easily from hither to yon (and beyond).

In this chapter, I'll give you the lowdown on these standards and show you how to best put them to practical use with your iPod and your computer's calendar application.

Va-va-va-vCal

To understand how your iPod handles appointments and events, it helps to know what's going on behind the scenes.

A little history

Flip back a chapter, and you'll learn that during the 1990s, the Versit group created the vCard standard. Undoubtedly, as this group clapped itself on the back for a job well done, one member interrupted with an "Ahem, excuse me, but since the bus to the airport won't be here for another hour, what say we hammer together a standard for swapping calendar information as well?"

And thus were born the vCalendar and iCalendar standards.

vCal (as the vCalendar standard is affectionately known) is a format for exchanging calendar and scheduling information between vCal-aware applications and devices. (vCal-aware devices include Palm Computing devices and the iPod.) iCalendar (which lacks an affectionate nickname) is a format designed to exchange calendars on the Internet. You can recognize iCalendar files by their .ics file extension (mycalendar.ics, for example). The iPod can read both vCal and iCalendar files.

These standards were written to be platform-independent, meaning that you can use them on a variety of computers running an assortment of operating systems (Windows, the Mac OS, and Linux, for example).

Anatomy of a vCal file

Were you to open a very basic vCal file in a text editor, you'd see that it contains such information as the application you used to create the file (Apple's iCal or Microsoft Outlook, for example); your time zone (U.S. Pacific, for example); and the date, time, and duration of your appointment. These files can also contain alarm information (whether to display an audible or visual alarm, or both), notes, and attendees (those whom you've invited to your appointment).

Here are the contents of a vCard file I created with Apple's iCal calendar application:

```
BEGIN:VCALENDAR
CALSCALE:GREGORIAN
X-WR-TIMEZONE;VALUE=TEXT:US/Pacific
METHOD:PUBLISH
PRODID:-//Apple Computer\, Inc//iCal 1.0//EN
X-WR-CALNAME;VALUE=TEXT:Meeting
VERSION:2.0
BEGIN:VEVENT
SEQUENCE:10
DTSTAMP:20021109T223001Z
SUMMARY:My Appointment
UID:D26B4DF8-F432-11D6-82DE-00039366F0C4
ORGANIZER;CN=Bubba Jones:mailto:bubba@bubba.com
X-WR-ITIPSTATUSML;VALUE=TEXT:UNCLEAN
DTSTART;TZID=US/Pacific:20021109T160000
DURATION:PT1H30M
DESCRIPTION:Mention the goat?
END:VEVENT
END:VCALENDAR
```

The entries worth paying attention to are:

- **PRODID.** This entry is the name of the program you used to create the file.

- **DTSTAMP.** This entry is the date and time that you created the file. I created this file on November 9, 2002—thus, the 20021109 entry.

- **SUMMARY.** This entry is the name of my appointment.

- **ORGANIZER.** This event was created by my alter ego, Bubba Jones, so Bubba's name and email address are attached to the file.

- **DTSTART.** The event is scheduled for November 9, 2002, U.S. Pacific time at 4:00 p.m. (The T160000 entry indicates 4:00 p.m. on a 24-hour clock.)

- **DURATION.** This entry details how long the appointment lasts. In this case, my appointment is scheduled for an hour and a half.

- **DESCRIPTION.** Any notes you've created for the appointment follow the DESCRIPTION entry.

If you add an appointment to your iPod, this information will appear in the Event window:

- **The date of the appointment.** Displayed in day/month/year format—11 Jan 2003, for example.

- **The time and duration of the appointment.** Displayed as 4:00 - 5:30 PM, for example.

- **The name of the appointment.** If you've named it My Appointment in your computer's calendar application, so shall it be named on your iPod.

- **The attendees.** If you've added attendees to the appointment in your computer's calendar application, those names will appear next in the Event screen.

- **Notes.** Any notes you've entered on your computer will appear last in the Event screen.

 Visual and audible alarms are also transferred to your iPod. However, you'll see no indication in the Event screen—or anywhere else, for that matter—that such alarms exist (though you'll have a pretty good idea when the alarm goes off).

Working with Calendars

Now that you're more familiar with the underpinnings of calendars on your computer and iPod, you're all set to do something practical with them. In the following pages, I'll show you how to create calendars in common Macintosh and Windows applications and then move those calendars to your computer. I'll also reveal the steps for removing expired calendar events from your iPod.

Creating calendars

Apple would have looked mighty foolish to add calendaring capabilities to the iPod without also providing Mac users a calendar application. It did so by releasing iCal, a free, basic calendar application that runs under Mac OS X 10.2 and later.

If you have a Mac incapable of running Mac OS X 10.2, fear not; iCal isn't the only Macintosh application that's compatible with the iPod. Both Microsoft Entourage (part of Microsoft Office X for Macintosh) and Palm's Palm Desktop 4.x can also export iPod-compatible vCal files.

Windows users can create iPod-friendly calendar files, too. Unfortunately, they can't do so with an Apple application. Although iCal and the Windows iPod were announced in nearly the same breath, Apple didn't feel compelled to release a version of iCal for Windows. Fortunately, those Windows users who have a copy of Microsoft Office will discover that Outlook can export calendar files that are compatible with the iPod, as can Palm's Palm Desktop 4.x.

iCal (Mac OS X 10.2 or later)

iCal allows you to import both vCal and iCalendar files. It exports only iCalendar files. (Its inability to export vCal files is no great loss to iPod owners, however, as the iPod can read both formats.)

I don't intend to present you with a complete overview of iCal; I'll leave that to the author of *Secrets of iCal*. I will, however, offer you the basics, showing you how to create a calendar and make that calendar ready for transfer to your iPod. You'll start by creating an *event* (iCal's term for an appointment). Follow these steps:

1. If you're running Mac OS X 10.2 or later, download and install a copy of iCal, if you haven't already (*www.apple.com/ical*).

2. Launch iCal.

    You'll see that the iCal window is divided into three panes: Calendars (where your individual calendars are listed), the main view (where you view your calendar by month, week, or day), and the To Do pane (**Figure 6.1**).

3. Click the Home entry in the Calendars pane.

    iCal ships with two calendars: Home and Work. (You can create additional calendars by clicking the plus-sign (+) button at the bottom of the iCal window.) Right now, though, you're going to add an event to the Home calendar.

4. Click the Week button at the bottom of the iCal window to switch to Week view.

You can use any view you like. I suggest using Week view because it illustrates one of the easiest ways to create an event.

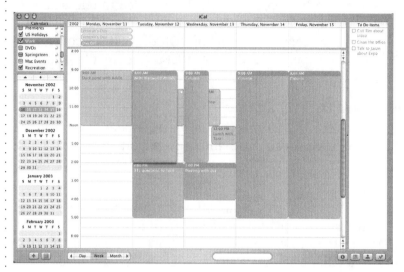

Figure 6.1 Apple's iCal.

5. Click and drag in a date column to create an event (**Figure 6.2**).

When you let go of your mouse, highlighted lettering appears within the event box.

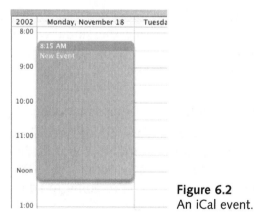

Figure 6.2
An iCal event.

6. Begin typing to name your event.

7. Rearrange the event to your satisfaction.

To move the event earlier or later in the day, for example, drag it to a new location. To move it to a different day, drag it to the day you desire. To adjust the length of the appointment, drag the top or bottom border of the event box.

8. Double-click inside the dark area at the top of your event to open the Event Info window (**Figure 6.3**).

Figure 6.3
An iCal Event Info
window.

In the panes within this window, you can adjust the date and time of your event, switch on audio and visual alarms, determine how often the event repeats (daily, weekly, monthly, or yearly), add invitees, and create notes.

Note that setting an iCal alarm to be visual-only has no bearing on how the iPod presents the alarm. When you configure the iPod to play an aural alarm (see the "Alarming Events" sidebar later in this chapter), the alarm will sound off even if you've created a visual-only alarm.

9. When the event is configured to your liking, feel free to create additional events.

10. To export your completed calendar, make sure that the Home calendar is still selected in the Calendars pane, and choose Export from the File menu.

11. In the resulting iCal: Export dialog box, select a destination for your calendar, give it a name, and click Export.

Your calendar is saved to the destination and ready to move to your iPod.

Microsoft Entourage (Mac OS X)

Microsoft Entourage, the email client and personal information manager application included with Microsoft Office X, offers more limited support for transportable calendar files than does iCal. Unlike iCal, Entourage doesn't allow you to export entire calendars. Rather, you can export only single events (and in not a terribly intuitive fashion). Here's how it works:

1. Launch Entourage, and click the Calendar button.

2. Select Week view in the toolbar at the top of the window.

You can use any view you like. I suggest using Week view because it illustrates one of the easiest ways to create an event.

3. Click and drag in a date column to create an event (**Figure 6.4**).

When you let go of your mouse, a range of time will be selected.

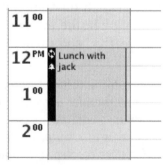

Figure 6.4
An Entourage event.

4. Double-click within this range to produce an untitled window where you can adjust the date and time of your event, schedule alarms, add notes, determine how often the event repeats, and add invitees (**Figure 6.5**).

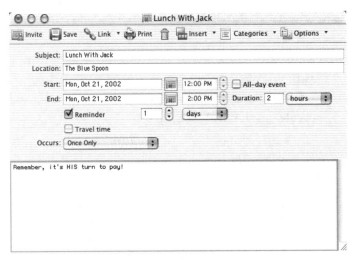

Figure 6.5 Inside an Entourage event.

5. Click the Save button at the top of the window to save your event and close the window.

To move the event earlier or later in the day, drag it to a new location. To move it to a different day, drag it to the day you desire. To adjust the length of the appointment, drag the bottom border of the event box.

Entourage offers no command for exporting calendars or events. To create a file for your event, you must drag it from your calendar to the Mac's Desktop or into a Finder window, where it turns into a .ics file.

The version of Entourage included in Microsoft Office 2001 doesn't support vCal or iCalendar files.

Palm Desktop 4.x (Mac OS 9, Mac OS X)

Palm's free Palm Desktop offers vCal support in both the Mac OS 9 and OS X versions of the application, giving those who are using Apple's older operating system a chance to create calendars for their iPods. Regrettably, vCal files created with Palm Desktop don't display Notes or Invitees information on the iPod. Creating calendars with both the Mac OS 9 and Mac OS X versions works the same way. Here's how to do it:

1. Download and install a copy of Palm Desktop (*www.palm.com/software/desktop/mac.html*).

2. Launch Palm Desktop, and select Date Book in the toolbar.

3. Click the Week tab in the Date Book window.

   You can use any view you like. I suggest using Week view because it illustrates one of the easiest ways to create an event.

4. Click and drag in a date column to create an event (**Figure 6.6**).

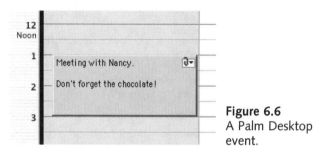

Figure 6.6
A Palm Desktop event.

5. In the resulting event window, name your event.

6. Double-click the event to open the Event window, where you can adjust the date and time of your event, schedule alarms, and determine how often the event repeats (**Figure 6.7**).

Figure 6.7 The makings of a Palm Desktop event.

Unlike its counterparts in iCal and Entourage, the Palm Desktop Event window doesn't allow you to designate invitees or add notes to your event. Although you can add contacts and memos to a Palm Desktop event, that information doesn't transfer to the iPod. For this reason, if you use Palm Desktop, you should type notes and contact information after the name of the event.

7. Click OK after you've configured the event to your liking.

    To move the event earlier or later in the day, drag it to a new location. To move it to a different day, drag it to the day you desire. To adjust the length of the appointment, drag the bottom border of the event box.

8. Move events, if you so desire.

You can move events out of Palm Desktop in two ways.

- The first way is simply to drag the event to the Mac's Desktop or a Finder window. When you do, the event is saved as a vCal (.vcs) file.

- The second way is to choose Export from Palm Desktop's File menu. In the Export: Palm Desktop dialog box, you'll have the opportunity to save your entire Date Book as a single vCal file. To do so, choose Date Book from the Module pop-up menu, All Datebook Items from the Items pop-up menu, and vCal from the Format pop-up menu (**Figure 6.8**). Name your file, and click the Export button.

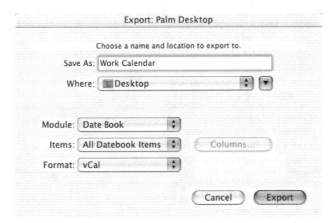

Figure 6.8 Use these settings to export a Palm Desktop Date Book as a vCal file.

iCal: The Easier Way

Given that iCal is a snap to use, and that you can use it to export entire calendars to your iPod, why shouldn't Mac users abandon these other applications and use iCal exclusively?

You may be reluctant to do so because all your appointments are already in Entourage or Palm Desktop. Or you may prefer the additional features in these other applications.

Far be it for me to muck with the way you organize your life, but may I suggest that if you intend to use your iPod extensively as your mobile calendar-keeper, you consider switching to iCal—even if only as a conduit for moving data from the other applications to your iPod? If you employ iCal (and Apple's device-synchronization application, iSync), you will find it much easier to move both your contacts and calendars on and off your iPod.

Moving appointments from Entourage and Palm Desktop to iCal is not difficult. Here's how:

Entourage. To import calendar events into iCal from Entourage, choose Import from iCal's File menu. In the resulting Import dialog box, you'll see the Import Entourage Data option. Select this option, and click Import (**Figure 6.9**).

Figure 6.9 Import Entourage events into iCal.

If it isn't already open, Entourage will launch, appearing as the frontmost application. Nothing will appear to happen for a while (perhaps for as long as an hour, if you have a lot of appointments and to-do items), but don't give up. Eventually, iCal will come to the fore, and your Entourage data will appear in the Entourage calendar that is now listed in iCal's Calendars pane.

Palm Desktop. Now you know that you can export events in Palm Desktop's Date Book as a single vCal file. Do so. When you have the exported file in hand, launch iCal, and choose Import from the File menu. Select the Import a vCal File option, and, in the resulting dialog box, navigate to the vCal file you exported from Palm Desktop. The data in the vCal file will be imported into the currently selected calendar.

Outlook (Microsoft Windows)

Microsoft's ubiquitous Outlook supports both vCal and iCalendar files, though not all the information you enter in an Outlook appointment will appear on your iPod. Here's the Windows way:

1. Launch Outlook, and click the Calendar button.

2. Choose any view you like, right-click the date you want to add an event to, and choose Add Appointment from the contextual menu.

3. In the resulting Untitled - Appointment window, adjust the day and time of your appointment, schedule alarms, and determine how often the event repeats (by clicking the Recurrence button; **Figure 6.10**).

   Although Outlook has a couple of places where it appears that you can include invitees in your appointment, those invitees will not appear in the calendar item on your iPod.

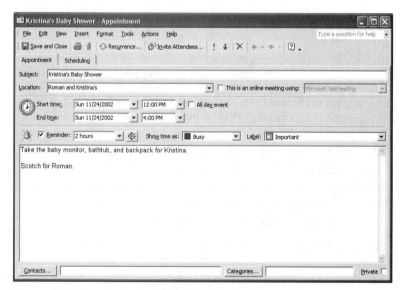

Figure 6.10 An Outlook Appointment window.

4. When the appointment is configured to your satisfaction, save and close the appointment.

   In Day and Work Week view, you can alter the date and time of your event by dragging the event. To move the event earlier or later in the day, drag it to a new location. To move it to a different day, drag it to the day you desire. To adjust the length of the appointment, drag the top or bottom border of the event box.

5. Click an appointment, and choose Save As from the File menu.

6. In the resulting Save As dialog box, choose iCalendar format from the Save As Type pop-up menu, name your file, and click Save (**Figure 6.11**).

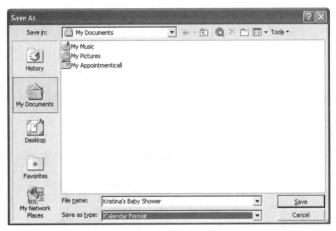

Figure 6.11 Use these settings to save an Outlook appointment as an iCalendar file.

Two notes: Why not save your file in the vCalendar format that's also offered in this pop-up menu? If you save your Outlook appointment as a vCal file, the alarms don't work on the iPod. Appointments saved in the iCalendar format broadcast their iPod alarms as they should.

And as tempting as it may be to pretend you're using a Mac and drag an Outlook appointment to the Desktop, don't bother. If you do, you'll create an Outlook file that your iPod can't read.

Palm Desktop 4.x (Microsoft Windows)

Palm Desktop 4.x for Windows works much the same way as it does on the Macintosh. Where it differs is in its ability to include notes that the iPod can read and its inability to transfer working alarms to the iPod. Here's how to set it up:

1. Download and install Palm Desktop (*www.palm.com/software/desktop*).

2. Launch Palm Desktop, and click the Calendar button.

3. Click the Week tab in the Date Book window.

   You can use any view you like. I suggest using Week view because it illustrates one of the easiest ways to create an event.

4. Click and drag in a date column to create an event.

5. In the resulting event window, name your event.

6. Double-click the event to open the Edit Event window.

   In the General tab, you can adjust the date and time of your event and schedule alarms (**Figure 6.12**).

Figure 6.12
Editing a Palm Desktop event.

To schedule repeating events, click the Repeat tab, and specify how often you want the event to repeat. To add a note to your event, click the Note tab, and type your text (**Figure 6.13**).

As with the Macintosh version of the program, you can't attach invitees to events and expect them to appear within a calendar event on your iPod.

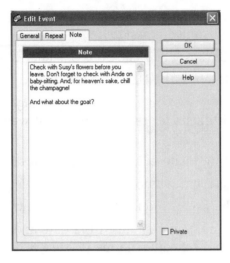

Figure 6.13
Why doesn't the Mac version of Palm Desktop offer a Notes window?

7. When you've finished editing your event, click OK.

   To move the event earlier or later in the day, drag it to a new location. To move it to a different day, drag it to the day you desire. To adjust the length of the appointment, drag the triangle that appears at the bottom of the event.

8. To export your event, select it and choose Export vCal from the File menu.

9. In the resulting Export As dialog box, name your file, and click Export.

   As I hinted earlier, the vCal files exported from Palm Desktop for Windows don't create alarms that work on the iPod. Regrettably, unlike with Outlook, there's no way to save Palm Desktop events as .ics files (which play alarms correctly).

Alarming Events

With all this talk of alarms, you may wonder exactly how alarms work on your iPod. Allow me to reveal all.

To begin with, if you expect your iPod to play or display alarms, you have to tell it to do so. The means for communicating your desire is the Alarms entry in the iPod's Settings screen.

The Alarms entry has three settings—Off, Silent, and On—that you cycle through by selecting Alarms and repeatedly pressing the Select key. By default, Alarms are set to On. This means that your alarm will beep and display an alarm message. (This message won't disappear until you press the Select button.) Note, however, that this beep emerges from inside the iPod and is *not* played through the iPod's sound port. That's why the displayed alarm message doesn't go away until you press Select. Should you miss the aural alert, a single glance at the iPod's active display will tell you that an alarm has gone off. (Don't worry—alert messages won't keep your iPod awake and, thus, deplete your battery. If you haven't dismissed the alarm message when the iPod goes to sleep, it will appear on screen when you next awaken your iPod.)

When you select Silent in the Alarms entry, your iPod won't emit its little beep to alert you when an alarm event occurs. Instead, the iPod displays the alert message only. This is a good option to choose if you take your iPod to places where a shrill-ish alarm would be unappreciated (movie theaters, restaurants, and church services, for example).

And the Off alarm setting tells the iPod to pay no mind to alarms attached to your calendar events.

Manually transferring calendars to the iPod

Now that you have all these calendar files, you should do something useful with them. To add them to your iPod manually, follow these steps:

1. Plug your iPod into your computer, and wait for it to mount.

    The iPod icon will appear on the Mac's Desktop or in Windows' My Computer window.

2. Double-click the iPod icon, and keep an eye peeled for the Calendars folder (**Figure 6.14**).

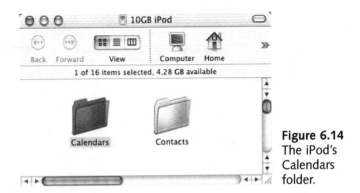

Figure 6.14
The iPod's
Calendars
folder.

3. Drag your calendar files to this Calendars folder.

4. Unmount your iPod, and unplug it.

5. When the main screen appears, scroll down to Extras, press Select, scroll to the Calendar entry, and press Select again.

   If you've moved multiple iCal calendars to your iPod, the screen you see will contain a list of those calendars (Home, Work, and Billy's Aussie Rules Football Schedule, for example). Scroll to the calendar you want to view, and press Select. In the next window, you'll see an overview of the current month. Those days that include events will be marked with a single black dot. (Days that contain multiple events don't display multiple dots.)

   If your iPod doesn't contain multiple calendars, when you press Select with the Calendars item highlighted, you'll be taken directly to the screen that displays the overview of the current month.

6. To view the appointments on a particular day, scroll to the date of the appointment, and press Select.

   In the next window, a list of appointments for that day appears.

7. Scroll to the appointment you want to view, and press Select again.

   The details of that appointment will be displayed in the iPod's Event screen.

There's no way to move from month to month immediately (but wouldn't it be swell if, in some future update, pushing the Fast Forward and Rewind buttons moved you forward or back a month?). To move through the year, you must scroll through every day on the calendar. Those who are even mildly fleet of thumb will find this easy to do.

Manually removing calendars from the iPod

Unless you make a habit of alienating your business associates, friends, and family, you probably don't need to remove contacts from your iPod routinely. Calendar items, on the other hand, are a different story. That lunch you had with your cousin last March 28th is now a dim memory (except for the fact that he stuck you with the check *again*) and could easily be expunged from your iPod's memory.

To do so, follow these steps:

1. Plug your iPod into your computer, and wait for it to mount.

   The iPod icon will appear on the Mac's Desktop or in Windows' My Computer window.

2. Double-click the iPod icon, and keep an eye peeled for the Calendars folder.

3. Open the Calendars folder, and drag the appropriate vCal or .ics file out of the folder (and into the Trash or Recycle Bin, if you like; **Figure 6.15**).

   The events associated with that file will no longer appear on your iPod.

Figure 6.15
Drag calendar files out of the iPod's Calendars folder to remove events from your iPod.

Before you remove one of these files, however, you should bear in mind that if a vCal or .ics file contains multiple events, trashing that file might obliterate both past and future appointments. For this reason, it's always a good idea to know exactly what a file contains before trashing it. One way to avoid doing The Bad Thing is to update your calendar on your computer and then replace the calendar file on your iPod with an updated version. (Apple's iSync and some Windows utilities I discuss just a little bit later can do this for you.)

You needn't worry that a load of calendars is going to overburden your iPod. Even if you're among the busiest of beavers, a year full of appointments and accompanying notes will create a calendar file far smaller than a single four-minute MP3 file. For this reason, you may choose to keep your old appointments on your iPod. This practice can come in handy at tax time, when you're tallying the past year's entertainment and travel expenses.

Automatically transferring calendars to the iPod

The manual methods for moving calendars on and off your iPod are hardly backbreaking, but why bother dragging files out of applications and into folders when a utility can do the job for you? Such utilities are available for users of both the Mac and Windows iPod.

iSync (Mac OS X 10.2 and later)

As much as I'd love to offer you a thicker book by reprinting the iSync material from Chapter 5, I'd feel guilty knowing that a few more trees met a pulpy end because of it. On the other hand, I hate to force you to flip back and forth from chapter to chapter, should you have read Chapter 5 when you were particularly sleepy. With that in mind, allow me to refresh your memory by providing these short-and-sweet instructions for using iSync to move iCal calendar events to your iPod:

1. Launch iSync.

2. If your calendars aren't in iCal, import them, using the methods I described earlier.

3. Mount your iPod.

4. If the iPod doesn't appear in iSync, add it by choosing the Add Device command from iSync's File menu.

5. Click the iPod's icon in the iSync window.

6. Be sure the Contacts check box is checked and that you've selected the calendars you want to place on your iPod (**Figure 6.16**).

Figure 6.16
Select the calendars you want to synchronize with iSync.

7. Click the Sync Now button.

Windows utilities

Yes, I gave away the plot for these utilities in Chapter 5 as well. The four Windows utilities I mention that allow you to move your Outlook contacts to the iPod easily—iPod Sync, iAppoint, OutPod, and EphPod—can also transfer Outlook calendar events to your iPod. Try 'em and see!

Accessories

7

Accessories. What accessories? Everything you need to operate the iPod comes in the box, right?

iPod... Check.

Headphones... Check.

Foam covers for those headphones... Check.

Software... Check.

Power adapter... Check.

FireWire cable... Check.

Remote control in 10 and 20 GB models... Check.

Carrying case in 10 and 20 GB models... Check.

Instructions... Check.

Other paperwork... Check.

What else could you possibly need?

In all likelihood, it won't be until you prepare to exploit the portable portion of the iPod's personality that you'll consider this question seriously. And then, consider it you shall.

"Gee, the clip on this Apple case doesn't seem very sturdy. I mean, if I twist it like this, and...*oops!*"

or

"Hmm. I suppose I could put this 5 GB iPod in my front pocket with my keys and loose coins, but I'll bet the shiny back scratches pretty easily."

or

"Man, I'd love to play these tunes in my car and on my home stereo, but how am I supposed to make the connection?"

or

"Whoa! I've got a long road trip ahead of me, and I'm not sure I can afford to stop for an hour at a gas station every time I want to recharge the iPod's battery."

or

"Ouch! The size of my ear canals must fall outside the norm. These earbuds don't fit at all!"

So although Apple does include everything you need to get started with the iPod, what is included is only a start. To incorporate the iPod into your active life completely, you need more. And more is exactly what I'll discuss in this chapter.

The Clip-On iPod

It didn't take long after the first iPods shipped for iPod owners to notice the effect gravity can have on objects dropped from an inverted shirt pocket. These same owners undoubtedly noticed that when an unprotected iPod shared accommodations with a pants-pocketful of loose change and keys, the iPod's shiny metal back came out worse for the wear.

Having paid careful attention to these concerns, Apple now issues cases with its 10 and 20 GB iPods. (By default, 5 GB iPods remain unprotected, though you can purchase the case separately for $39.) Although it's stylish and provides a fair measure of protection, this case requires that you remove the iPod to access the front-panel controls (not a terrible burden, considering that the 10 and 20 GB models also ship with the remote control), and the case bears a clip that is too easy to break.

So if Apple's iPod case doesn't measure up, what should one look for in a case?

What to look for

A good case should offer the following features (**Figure 7.1** and **Figure 7.2**):

- A system for attaching the iPod to your body (a belt clip or strap, for example)
- Construction sturdy enough to protect the iPod from scratches
- A place to store the iPod's earbuds and remote control

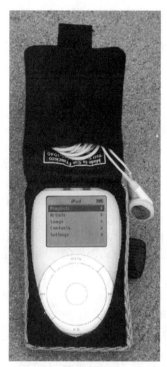

Figure 7.1
Waterfield Designs' Super Dooper iPod Case has all the features you'd look for in an iPod case: padding, easy access to controls and ports, a belt clip, and stylish design.

Figure 7.2
Detachable belt clips are mighty convenient.

These features are the bare minimum you should expect from your case. Frankly, with a piece of bubble wrap, a clothespin, and a couple of pieces of duct tape, you could construct a case that meets these requirements. Looking beyond the essentials, what else might you look for?

- A way to detach the iPod from your body easily

At times, you'll want to fiddle with the iPod—adjust the volume, flick on the Hold switch, or use the controls to skip a song. You'll find it more convenient to do so if you don't have to detach some elaborate harness or use a pair of pliers to pry apart a belt clip. Look for the kind of quick-release clip you find on many of today's cellular-phone cases.

- A way to access the controls easily

Although the remote control has made access to the controls less necessary than it was during the pre-remote-control days, at times you'll still need to punch and scroll around the face of the iPod—particularly when you're searching for contact or calendar information. A case that opens in the front will make these kinds of operations far more convenient. You should also be able to access the audio jack—and, ideally, the FireWire port and hold switch—without having to disassemble the case.

- Design sturdy enough to provide your iPod a reasonable chance of survival, should you drop it

Although an unscratched iPod has its aesthetic benefits, little good it does you if it won't play because you've dropped the poor thing and broken it. The iPod is fairly robust, but it won't hurt to give it a helping hand by swaddling it in a well-padded case.

- Design that makes a statement

Let's face it—you dropped a lot of cash on your iPod. There are far cheaper (and less elegant) music players on the market. Do you really want to encase this jewel in a shoddy-looking case? The iPod is cool. It deserves a cool case.

On the cases

Realizing that there was a crying need for iPod cases, several companies produced some worthwhile products. Following are a few of my favorites.

Super Dooper iPod Case
www.sfbags.com

Waterfield Designs' $40 Super Dooper iPod Case meets all the aforementioned criteria. It features a quick-release clip that releases only if you turn the case to the side (to prevent accidental unclipping), a padded front panel that flips up to give you complete access to the iPod's front controls, and a slit top that allows you to reach the ports and switch on the top of the iPod. It's a stylish, mostly-black case that comes with red, white, or blue highlights (refer to Figures 7.1 and 7.2).

SportSuit and C.E.O Classic cases
www.marware.com

Marware makes two models of the SportSuit case. Both fit all iPod models.

The $40 SportSuit Convertible Case includes a shaped lid suitable for storing your earbuds; you can flip up this lid to access the iPod's controls. You can also get to the ports and switch at the top of the iPod without lifting the lid. The case includes a flexible belt-clip system that allows you to remove the clip and attach an armband, belt, bike holder, car holder, or lanyard. (The basic package includes the belt clip and armband.) The design features a reinforced back and sides, and the lid is sturdy enough to protect the face of the iPod. It's a good-looking case that comes in black, navy (dark blue), blue (wetsuit blue), gray, red, and yellow.

The $20 SportSuit Sleeve is a much more basic case. It includes a nondetachable rotating belt clip, a pouch for your earbuds, a neoprene exterior (with vulcanized neoprene sides), and a top flap that provides a single hole for access to the audio jack. To access the controls, you have to remove the iPod from the case. It comes in the same colors as the SportSuit Convertible Case.

The $35 C.E.O. Classic case (which fits only 5 and 10 GB iPods) has everything you'd want in a case: easy access to the front controls and top ports, adequate padding, a plastic screen protector, storage on the lid, and a flexible clip system. (You can put a variety of clips on the thing.) The one drawback is that it comes in a single style: black leather. If you're a vegan or looking for a more colorful case, you'll need to look elsewhere.

Deluxe iPod Case
www.xtrememac.com

XtremeMac's Deluxe iPod Case may be the most accessory-rich iPod case on the planet. The $30 basic model features a reinforced flip-up cover, a clear Mylar front cover to protect the controls (you can use the controls with the cover in place), access to the top ports and switch, a detachable belt clip, and a clip-on pouch for your earbuds. The case comes in 13 styles; in materials such as leather and suede, and in patterns ranging from basic black to lavender to leopard skin.

More extensive bundles priced between $40 and $50 include a neck lanyard, swivel-mount clips, and a car charger for your iPod.

iSee
www.contourdesign.com

If you'd like to show off your iPod even when it's tucked snugly into its case, check out Contour Design's completely clear, $25 iSee case. The case provides access to the ports and controls; it features a low-profile clip and four small plastic feet on the back of the case (a nice idea if you don't want your iPod skittering across an airplane tray table). Accompanying the iSee is a small white plastic case for the headphones.

The iSee lacks padding, so this isn't the case to use if you intend to drop your iPod on a regular basis. As I write this chapter (in late 2002), iSee is available for only the 5 and 10 GB iPods.

And others
Although there's a certain cachet to owning a case designed specifically for the iPod, less-expensive—and, perhaps, more-appropriate—solutions are available.

The Original Tune Belt Cassette Player Carrier
www.tunebelt.com

Suppose that you want to take your iPod jogging, to the gym, or on a bike ride. An iPod clipped to your belt may just get in the way. What you might find more suitable is a fanny-pack arrangement such as the one provided by The Original Tune Belt Cassette Player Carrier (**Figure 7.3**). As the name implies, this $15 neoprene carrier belt was designed to hold a portable cassette player, but there's nothing to keep you from packing your iPod into it. Just press the iPod's Play button, shove the iPod into the pouch, belt on the carrier, and start working that cardiovascular system.

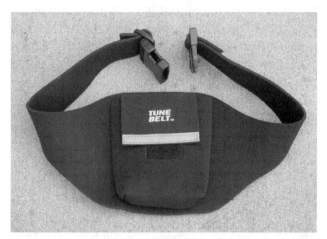

Figure 7.3 Active iPod users might be interested in the clip-on Tune Belt.

No, you won't have easy access to the front controls, and there are no special holes cut into the thing for earbud access, but when you're on a cross-country bike ride, you really shouldn't be taking your hands off the handlebars to fiddle with the iPod's controls anyway.

The "anything's better than nothing" solution
A quick crawl through the local electronics mart will reveal lots of other ways to protect your iPod. That padded PDA case will do in a pinch, or perhaps the generic $12 MP3 and Mini-Disc player case would work. And if you just want something to keep your iPod from being scratched when you throw it into your backpack, how about that cheap camera case?

The fact is, if you don't care about access or style, you can put your iPod in anything more robust than a paper bag that will accommodate a standard deck of playing cards. Only you know how much abuse you're going to direct at your iPod and the level of protection you need.

Adaptive Technology

Although the iPod's audio jack is labeled with the headphones symbol, that jack can accommodate more than the iPod's ear-buds. Unlike the headphone jack on some other electronic devices, the iPod's audio jack can send out perfectly clean audio from this port to your computer's sound input port or to a home or car stereo. All you need to perform this feat is the right cable. In this section, I'll show you exactly which cables to use and how to string them properly from the iPod to the device of your choice (**Figure 7.4**).

Figure 7.4
Make connections with your iPod with these common audio connectors, which include (from left to right) RCA connectors, a female miniplug jack, and a male miniplug.

iPod to computer

You already know that if you want to swap data between your iPod and Mac or PC, you use a FireWire cable. But in some instances, you may want to record directly from your iPod to your computer. To do so, you need an adapter cable that carries stereo Walkman-style miniplugs on both ends. (You can distinguish a stereo miniplug from the mono variety by the two black bands on the plug. A mono miniplug has just one black band.)

Just plug one end of the cable into the iPod's audio jack and the other into your computer's audio input port. (Note: Audio input ports are missing from some Mac models. For these Macs, you need a USB audio adapter, such as Griffin Technology's $35 iMic audio adapter.) To record audio from the iPod on your computer, you'll need some variety of audio-editing application. When you have that application installed properly, click the Record button in that program and then press the iPod's Play button. The iPod's audio will be recorded on the computer.

You can find such cables at your local electronics boutique for less than $5 for a 6-foot cable. Higher-quality cables that include better shielding, thicker cable, and gold connectors can cost significantly more.

iPod to home stereo

Take the *personal* out of *personal music player* by attaching your iPod to your home stereo and subjecting the rest of the household to your musical whims. You need nothing more than a cable that features a stereo miniplug on one end and two mono RCA plugs on the other.

Plug the miniplug into the iPod's audio jack and the two RCA plugs into an input on your stereo receiver (the AUX input, for example). With this arrangement, you can control the volume not only with your stereo's volume control, but with the iPod's scroll wheel as well.

A cheap version of this cable also costs less than $5. Griffin Technology (*www.griffintechnology.com*) offers the $15 ClearChoice iPod Connection Kit, which includes a high-quality version of this cable—a 4-foot miniplug-to-male RCA adapter cable—along with a cable that features a pair of female RCA plugs and a stereo miniplug. The cables are iPod-color-coordinated and carry gold-plated connectors. With the first cable, you can connect your iPod to your stereo. Using the cables in tandem, you can connect your iPod to your computer or to computer speakers that carry female miniplug connectors for input.

iPod to hard-wired computer speakers

Some computer speakers are *hard-wired,* meaning that the manufacturer, in its cheapskate wisdom, decided to save a couple of pennies by attaching the speaker cable permanently to the speaker. To connect your iPod to such speakers, you need a cable that features a male stereo miniplug on one end and a female miniplug on the other. To make the connection, plug the adapter cable's male miniplug into the iPod's audio port and the speaker's male miniplug into the female miniplug connector on the other end of the adapter cable.

Inexpensive versions of these cables also cost less than $5 and are available at your local electronics boutique.

iPod to two headphones

There may (and I hope there *will*) come a time when you want to snuggle up with your snookums and listen to your Special Song played on an iPod. A touch of romance goes out of this ritual, however, when you have to split a pair of earbuds between you and your li'l sweet potato.

To bring the intimacy back to your musical relationship, purchase a stereo line splitter. Such an adapter bears a single stereo male miniplug connector on one end (the end you plug into the iPod) and two stereo female miniplug connectors on the other. Plug a pair of headphones into each female connector, and you're set. (Well, you're *almost* set; you still get to argue about who controls the volume.)

XtremeMac (*www.xtrememac.com*) sells such a connector, called the iShare Earbud Splitter, for $10. Belkin (*www.belkin.com*) offers a Headphone Splitter Cable for $8, available at both the bricks-and-mortar and virtual Apple Stores. You'll find similar adapters at your local electronics bazaar.

iPod to car stereo

This one's a bit trickier. A few car stereos include a miniplug jack labeled *CD*. If you have such a jack, you're in luck. Just use a stereo miniplug-to-miniplug cable (like the one I recommend for the iPod-to-computer connection), and you're ready to rock. If you don't have a connector, a technician at a Ye Olde Auto Stereo Shoppe may be able to provide one by tapping into a hidden connector on the back of the car stereo. If taking your car to such a tech sounds like a bother, though, you might try one of these adapters.

Cassette-player adapter

If your car has a cassette player, you can use a cassette adapter (**Figure 7.5**). These things look exactly like audio cassettes, save for the thin cable that trails from the back edge of the adapter. To use one of these adapters, shove the adapter into your car's cassette player, plug its cable into your iPod, and press the Play buttons on both the iPod and the cassette player. Music should issue from your car's speakers.

These adapters cost less than $20.

Figure 7.5
A cassette adapter allows you to play your iPod through a cassette player.

Although you can use these adapters in any cassette player—a boom box or home stereo, for example—you may have some difficulty ejecting the adapter from players that feature snap-down doors. The adapter's cable may wedge between the door and the inside of the player, making it difficult to open the door.

Wireless music adapter

Cassette adapters are fine as long as your car has a working cassette player and you don't mind having a cable trailing from your player to wherever you place your iPod. But if you lack such a player (or just can't stand the untidiness inherent with such adapters), consider a wireless music adapter (**Figure 7.6**).

This small, battery-operated device works like a tiny radio station, broadcasting whatever is plugged into it to a nearby FM radio. Some of these devices offer you the choice to switch among a few frequencies in the college radio and National Public Radio range—88.1, 88.3, 88.5, and 88.7 MHz, for example—whereas others provide a dial so that you can fine-tune reception. These devices work in a very limited range. Move them more than a couple of feet from the radio's antenna, and you'll pick up interference. For this reason, they're not ideal for use with a home stereo. Their effectiveness in an automobile depends on how heavily populated the airwaves are around you. A strong radio signal will overpower these devices, rendering them ineffective. If you live in an urban area with a plethora of active radio stations (or plan to travel in one routinely), you may want to explore a hard-wired connection or a cassette adapter.

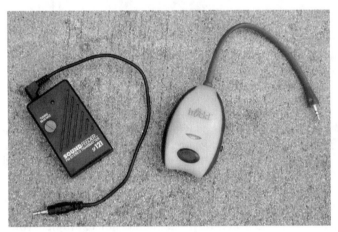

Figure 7.6 Play your iPod through your car's FM radio with one of these wireless music adapters.

iRock (*www.myirock.com*) makes the $30 iRock! 300W Wireless Music Adapter, which features a cool design, requires two AAA batteries (should last for about 20 hours of use), and includes a selector switch that lets you choose among four frequencies.

Arkon Resources (*www.arkon.com*) makes the diminutive $25 SoundFeeder SF121 FM Stereo Transmitter. This device also requires two AAA batteries and includes a dial that allows you to select any channel between 88 and 95MHz.

TransPod

The $100 TransPod, from Everythingipod.com is the automotive all-in-one solution (*www.everythingipod.com*). The device is comprised of a mounting bracket that you attach to a convenient location on your car's dashboard, a power adapter, and an FM transmitter. When you slide your iPod into the bracket, the TransPod pulls power from the car's cigarette-lighter receptacle (now labeled a power receptacle in many cars) and is ready to broadcast to a user-designated FM radio station.

Having It All

Given the number of ways you can accessorize your iPod, you may think that you'll spend a fair amount of time ordering online or hopping from shop to shop to get everything you need. Relax—there's an easier way.

Dr. Bott LLC (**www.drbott.com**) provides just about everything you require in its iPod Connection Kits (**Figure 7.7**). The company's $45 iPod Connection Kit with FM Transmitter includes the SoundFeeder FM stereo transmitter (with two AAA batteries), an auto-charger adapter for charging your iPod from your car's cigarette lighter, a carrying pouch, and the three cables I list earlier in this chapter. The $40 iPod Connection Kit II with Tape Adapter substitutes a cassette-tape adapter for the FM transmitter.

XtremeMac.com offers its $50 Get Connected Bundle. This bundle includes a variety of adapter cables (including the iShare Earbud Splitter), an auto charger, and an audio cassette adapter.

Figure 7.7
Just what the doctor ordered: the Dr. Bott iPod Connection Kit II.

Power to the People

Like the heads of government, your iPod needs power to do its job. To bring power to your iPod, consider these accessories.

iPod Power Adapter

Apple included one of these with the iPod, correct? Correct. But the iPod is a portable music player, and if you routinely truck it between a couple of locations—your home and office, for example—it might be convenient to have a power adapter at each end of your journey. You can purchase an additional iPod Power Adapter at the online Apple Store (*http://store.apple.com*) for $49 (**Figure 7.8**).

Figure 7.8 It's twice as nice to have an extra Apple iPod Power Adapter.

FireJuice

SiK's $27 FireJuice (*www.sik.com*) is a very adaptable power adapter (**Figure 7.9**). The adapter features a switch that lets you use external power (an iPod AC adapter or auto adapter, for example), no power, or power from the computer's FireWire port. The FireWire data connection is always on.

Figure 7.9 The iPod's most adaptable adapter, FireJuice.

Why would you want such a feature? As you may recall, you can't charge an iPod from an unpowered FireWire port—a port on a FireWire PC card or a four-pin FireWire PCI card, for example. The FireJuice adapter makes it possible to charge your iPod when it's connected to such an unpowered port. Those who are using their iPods with a PowerBook or iBook running on battery power would set the FireJuice to the "no power" position so the iPod wouldn't attempt to charge from the laptop's battery during syncing (thus saving precious battery life on the laptop).

Auto charger

That extra iPod Power Adapter is so much useless metal and plastic when you're in a car miles from the nearest electrical outlet. To keep your iPod topped off on the road, you need an auto charger. The device plugs into your car's cigarette lighter or 12-volt receptacle, and power is delivered to your iPod through a plug that fits in the iPod's FireWire port (**Figure 7.10**).Both Dr. Bott (*www.drbott.com*) and Griffin Technology (*www.griffintechnology.com*) make auto chargers. Dr. Bott's Auto Charger for iPod costs $25; it includes a power indicator and a replaceable fuse to protect the iPod should too much juice slip through the adapter.

Figure 7.10 Keep your iPod charged on the road with an auto charger.

Griffin Technology's PowerPod Auto Adapter costs $20, and also includes a power indicator and replaceable fuse. Unlike the charger from Dr. Bott, this charger allows you to detach the FireWire cable from the PowerPod, so you can use a single FireWire cable for powering your iPod in the car, powering it from Apple's iPod Power Adapter, and connecting it to your Mac.

SiK's Auto Adapter iPod is a $21 auto charger that also includes a power indicator and replaceable fuse. Its 4-foot cable is thinner than the cable on some other adapters, thus putting less stress on the iPod's FireWire port.

Note that with these adapters, you can play your iPod while it's charging.

HotWire

Have you ever been frustrated that you can't listen to your iPod when it's plugged into the iPod Power Adapter? End that frustration with SiK's $16 HotWire cable. This power-only cable allows you to have full access to your iPod's controls while the iPod charges, so you can play your iPod during the process.

The Ears Have It

The iPod's earbuds are among the finest of their kind. But this style of headphone is inherently problematic, because (a) not all ear canals are the same size, so a one-size-fits-all set of earbuds may not fit all and (b) some people get the heebie-jeebies when items are lodged inside their ears. For these reasons, your list of accessories may include an additional set of headphones. Headphones come in a variety of styles—including earbuds, neckband, open-air, and closed—from such companies as Etymotic, Sony, Koss, Aiwa, Panasonic, Philips, and Sennheiser.

Earbuds

If you like earbud-style headphones but find those included with the iPod (**Figure 7.11**) to be uncomfortable (particularly if you have the original earbuds that were considered by many to be too big), earbuds are available from a variety of manufacturers. Look for earbuds that fit well, don't require a lot of fiddling to focus (meaning that you don't have to move them around continually to make them sound good), and offer reasonably well-balanced sound.

Figure 7.11 The iPod includes a set of earbud-style headphones.

The absolute top-of-the-line in-ear headphones are produced by Etymotic (*www.etymotic.com*). If sound quality is of paramount importance to you (and you have a fair chunk of disposable income), check out the $330 ER-4S earphones.

Neckband headphones

These popular headphones are secured to your head with wires that drape over the tops of your ears. Imagine putting on a pair of tight glasses backward, so that the lenses are on the back of your head, and you'll get the idea (**Figure 7.12**). Neckband headphones are comfortable but easy to dislodge if you tug on the cable. Also, they don't provide a lot of sound isolation, which means that sounds from outside tend to filter through. (This isn't necessarily a bad thing if someone's trying to get your attention or your smoke alarm goes off.)

Figure 7.12 Neckband headphones are easy to store and produce reasonable sound.

Open-air headphones

Open-air headphones sit over the ears without enclosing them completely (**Figure 7.13**). When you bought your portable CD or cassette player, open-air headphones likely were included in the box. These headphones are comfortable, but the less-expensive models can sound thin. Like neckband headphones, they don't provide much isolation.

Figure 7.13 Open-air headphones such as these are lightweight and comfortable.

Closed headphones

Closed headphones cover your ears completely and provide a lot of isolation, leaving you undistracted by outside sounds and those around you undisturbed by a lot of sound bleeding out of your headphones (**Figure 7.14**). Some closed headphones can be a bit bulky and uncomfortable, particularly if you wear glasses, so be sure to try before you buy. And because of their size, these headphones aren't terribly portable.

Figure 7.14
Closed headphones such as this Sony MDR-V6 model sound great but are bulky.

Shopping for Headphones

You wouldn't purchase a pair of stereo speakers without listening to them, would you? Of course not. It's just as important to audition a set of headphones that you intend to spend a lot of time with. When you're auditioning those headphones, keep the following factors in mind:

- **Sound quality.** A good set of headphones provides a nice balance of highs and lows without emphasizing one band of frequencies over another. Listen for a natural sound. If the headphones lack brightness—or if you can't clearly discern low-frequency instruments, such as bass guitar, cello, or a kick drum, and hearing your music clearly matters to you—move on. These aren't the headphones for you.

- **Comfort and fit.** If you're an enthusiastic listener, you may wear those headphones for long stretches of time. If they pinch your ears or head, or slip off every time you look down, you'll quickly grow tired of them.

- **Size.** Apple's earbuds not only sound great, but also are ultra-portable. If you plan to take your headphones with you, look for a pair that fits easily into a pocket or iPod case.

It's also a good idea to seek the opinions of others before purchasing a set of headphones. The HeadWize (**www.headwize.com**) Web site is a wonderful repository of information for headphone enthusiasts. Check HeadWize's forums for user reviews of popular (and more-obscure) headphones.

Miscellanea

And then there are the iPod accessories that defy categorization. If you've done the rest, try these accessories on for size.

iPod Remote

If you have a 10 or 20 GB iPod released after July 2002, you already have Apple's iPod Remote (**Figure 7.15**)—the company's wired remote control. If you have a 5 GB iPod or an earlier iPod model, the $39 iPod Remote is worth considering. It allows you to access the iPod's play controls without removing the device from a case or pocket. Very handy. The iPod Remote includes a set of Apple's earbuds.

Figure 7.15 After you've used the iPod Remote, you'll wonder how you listened without it.

PowerMate

Griffin Technology's $45 programmable USB audio and media controller, PowerMate, isn't exactly an iPod accessory, in the sense that you can't attach it directly to the iPod (**Figure 7.16**). You can, however, attach this jog-wheel controller to your Mac and use it to adjust your iPod's volume within iTunes.

Figure 7.16 Griffin Technology's Power-Mate audio controller.

Just attach the PowerMate to a free USB port, install the driver, and restart your Mac. Upon restart, launch iTunes; click your iPod in the Source list; open the iPod Preferences window; and select the Manually Manage Songs and Playlists option, which allows you to play your iPod through your Mac's speakers.

Then press down on the PowerMate to start playback, and turn the wheel up or down to adjust volume. Bonus: The PowerMate will perform these iTunes chores even when iTunes is not the active application.

iPodCradle and iPodDock

BookEndz's (*www.bookendzdocks.com*) $30 iPodCradle acts as a stand for your iPod that you place on your desk. The white plastic cradle tilts the iPod at a convenient viewing angle and can accommodate an iPod inside a standard case.

The $45 iPodDock (**Figure 7.17**) provides the same cradle function and also lets you connect your iPod to your Mac or home stereo easily. Just string a FireWire cable between your Mac and the Dock; string an audio cable between the Dock and an input on your home stereo; turn the iPod upside down; and shove it into the docking portion of the stand, where FireWire and audio connectors wait to complete the connection.

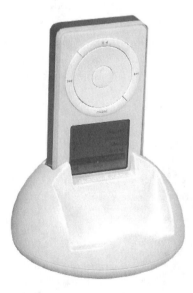

Figure 7.17
Connect your iPod to your Mac or home stereo easily with BookEndz's iPodDock.

The personalized iPod

What could personalize your personal music player more than having your name and favorite quote etched across the shiny back of your iPod (**Figure 7.18**)? For an additional $49, Apple will engrave the back of your iPod with two lines of text, comprised of 27 characters per line (and yes, spaces and punctuation count as characters), when you purchase your iPod from the online Apple Store (*http://store.apple.com*).

Figure 7.18
Apple will personalize
your iPod for $49.

Should you already own an iPod and desire this kind of personalization, try taking your iPod to a local jeweler. For the right price, a jeweler should be able to do the job for you.

Troubleshooting Your iPod

I regret to report that—except for you, dear reader, and me—nothing is perfect. No, not even the iPod. Whereas it may tick happily along one day, the next day, its menu structure is a mess; it refuses to start up when you're sure it has a full battery; or when it does start up, it displays an icon indicating that it is feeling far from well.

In this chapter, I'll look at the common maladies that afflict the iPod and what, if anything, you can do about them. I'll also examine the iPod's hidden diagnostic screen. Finally, I'll take you on a tour of the inside of an iPod and offer suggestions about when it might be a good idea to crack yours open.

Problems and Solutions

Unlike a computer that can fail in seemingly countless and creative ways, the iPod exhibits only a few behaviors when it's feeling poorly. Following are the most common problems and (when available) their solutions.

The missing Windows iPod

iPods rarely go missing on Macs but may fail to appear on Windows PCs. This absence is not due to a problem with the iPod, but to the relationship among the iPod, FireWire card, and Windows.

If the iPod refuses to mount on your Windows PC, make sure that your PC's FireWire (IEEE 1394) card is Windows Hardware Quality Labs (WHQL) certified. The literature that came with the card should indicate whether it's compliant. If not, check the vendor's Web site for compatibility information.

The confused iPod

Clues that your iPod is confused are the absence of playlists, artists, and songs that used to be there; a capacity that appears to be 5 GB on a 10 GB iPod; the failure of the iPod to boot beyond the Apple logo; or the appearance of a folder icon with an exclamation point. I'll look at each scenario in the following sections.

Absence of items

While I was attempting to use a Mac iPod with Windows, my PC crashed, and when I unplugged the iPod, its playlists were missing. I could still play music from the iPod through the Songs screen, but things were not right.

In an attempt to restore a sense of sanity to my iPod, I tried these remedies:

1. **Reset the iPod** (press and hold Play and Menu for 10 seconds).

    Resetting the iPod is similar to pushing the Reset switch on your Mac. It forces the iPod to restart and (ideally) get its little house in order. In this case, the iPod remained confused.

2. **Restore the iPod** (run the latest iPod Software Updater).

   If reset doesn't work, there's nothing else for it than to restore the iPod to its original factory state—meaning that all the data on it is removed. To restore the iPod on the Macintosh, launch the most recent copy of iPod Software Updater, and click the Restore button in the resulting window (**Figure 8.1**). Confirm that you want to restore by clicking Restore in the warning sheet (Mac OS X) or dialog box (Mac OS 9) that appears (**Figure 8.2**).

Figure 8.1 Click the Restore button in the iPod Software Updater window to begin the restore process.

Figure 8.2 Are you sure?

   To restore a Windows iPod, use the Start menu to navigate to the iPod folder inside the Program Files folder (**Figure 8.3**). Launch the Updater application, located inside the iPod folder. Then click the Restore button to begin the restoration process (**Figure 8.4**).

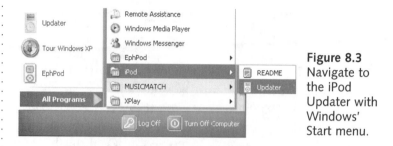

Figure 8.3
Navigate to
the iPod
Updater with
Windows'
Start menu.

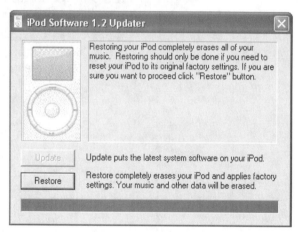

Figure 8.4 iPod Software 1.2 Updater in Windows.

Note that the Windows version of the Updater doesn't ask you to confirm your decision to restore the iPod. Be sure that you really want to restore the iPod before clicking the Restore button.

After the updater does its job, you must unplug and replug the iPod for the restore process to complete. After you replug the iPod, it will appear to restart several times. When the process is complete, the Updater window will return to its initial state, offering you the option to restore your iPod (**Figure 8.5**).

When you double-click your iPod's icon on the Mac's Desktop or in Windows' My Computer window, you'll see that the device contains only the Calendars and Contacts folder (with the sample contacts supplied by Apple).

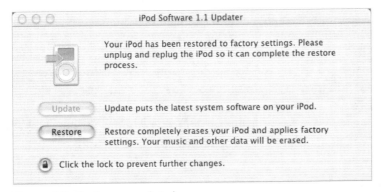

Figure 8.5 Restore completed.

To put your songs back on the Macintosh iPod, just launch iTunes and synch the iPod with iTunes.

When Windows users quit the Updater, MusicMatch Jukebox will launch and present the Device Setup window (**Figure 8.6**). You've undoubtedly seen this window in the past, but as a reminder, this window is where you can name your iPod, choose whether it will update all playlists or selected playlists when synchronized with MusicMatch Jukebox, choose to synchronize the iPod and MusicMatch Jukebox when the iPod is plugged into the PC, and enable the iPod for FireWire disk use.

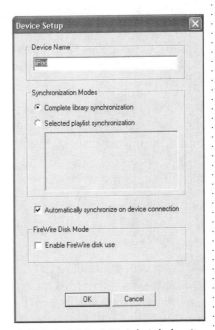

Figure 8.6 MusicMatch Jukebox's Device Setup window.

Incorrect capacity

This problem can occur when you've restored a Macintosh iPod with a software updater that's not intended for that device. The 10 GB iPod, for example, should be restored only with iPod Software 1.1 Updater or later. If you restore with the version 1.0.4 update, for example, your 10 GB iPod will be confused. Apple no longer offers this update online, so if the 10 GB iPod is your first iPod, you're highly unlikely to have this problem.

Failure to boot

There are a few possible reasons why an iPod might not boot beyond the Apple logo—some benign and others not so.

The Hold switch is on. Go ahead and smack yourself in the head (and then breathe a sigh of relief) if your iPod won't start up because the Hold switch is engaged.

Drained battery. Among the most benign problems is an iPod battery that's drained. If the iPod is functioning normally otherwise, when you attempt to switch on an iPod with a drained battery, you will see a message that reads, "No battery power remains. Please connect iPod to power." Plug your iPod into the power adapter or your computer, and let it charge. If everything's hunky-dory after that, pat yourself on the back for a job well done.

In some rare cases, the battery may not be drained enough for the iPod to be reset. If you've tried other solutions and failed, unplug the iPod from a power supply for 24 hours; then plug it into a power source and attempt to reset it by holding down the Play and Menu buttons for 10 seconds.

Confused iPod. If the iPod still refuses to boot, attempt to reset it by pressing and holding the Play and Menu buttons for 10 seconds.

Incorrect formatting. At some point, you might have thought it would be a nifty idea to reformat your iPod's hard drive—partitioned it on a Macintosh to install Mac OS 9 on one partition and Mac OS X on the other, for example. Or you've used a Windows utility other than the iPod Software Updater to format the drive. Bad idea. You should format the iPod only with the iPod Software Updater. To put things right, you must restore your iPod (see the "Restore the iPod" step in "Absence of items" earlier in this chapter).

> *As I mentioned in Chapter 4, there's nothing to keep you from formatting your Mac iPod as a Windows iPod, or vice versa. Just be sure that if you're subjecting your iPod to a platform change, you use the appropriate iPod Software Updater to do the job.*

Songs skip

Songs played on the iPod may skip for several reasons. They include:

Large song file. Large song files ("Mountain Jam" from the Allman Brothers' classic "Eat a Peach," for example) don't play particularly well with the iPod's 32 MB RAM buffer. Such large files race through the RAM buffer, requiring that the iPod access the hard drive more often. This can lead to skipping if the iPod is pulling the song almost directly from the hard drive. If possible, reduce the size of files by employing greater compression, or chop really long files into pieces.

Damaged file. A damaged song file may skip. If you find that the same song skips every time you play it—and other songs seem to play back with no problem—go back to the source of the song (an audio CD, for example), rip the song again, and replace the copy on the iPod with the newly ripped version.

iPod that needs to be reset. Yes, an iPod that needs to be reset may cause songs to skip.

iPod that needs to be restored. If a reset won't do the trick, make sure that all the data on your iPod is backed up, and restore the iPod with the latest version of iPod Software Updater.

Remote control doesn't work

The connection between the iPod and the remote control needs to be *very* snug. If your remote control isn't working, give the plug a good, hard push (and a twist) into the Sound Output port.

The really confused iPod

Your iPod may be so confused that it won't mount on your Mac's Desktop or in Windows' My Computer window and can't be restored. Follow these steps to mount the iPod:

1. Connect the iPod to a built-in FireWire port on your computer (rather than an unpowered FireWire port on a PC Card, for example).

2. Reset the iPod by pressing the Play and Menu buttons for 10 seconds.

3. When you see the Apple logo, press and hold the Previous and Next buttons until you see a message that reads "Do not disconnect." This key combination resets the iPod much like pressing the Reset switch on a PC or Mac resets the computer.

   With luck, your iPod should appear on the Mac's Desktop or in Windows' My Computer window. Then you should be able to restore it with the iPod Software Updater.

If you're using a version of the iPod Software Updater before version 1.2 (and this would be Macs only, because 1.2 was the first version to ship with the Windows models), don't be alarmed if you see a FireWire symbol instead of the "Do not disconnect" message in the iPod's display. The operation (and effect) are the same. Only the display is different.

Kelly's Sidebar: "Do not disconnect"

Shortly after Apple released the latest generation of iPods, my friend Kelly contacted me in what can be politely described as a state of concern. Our conversation went something like this:

She: "I can't disconnect my iPod from my computer! I thought this was supposed to be a *portable* music player!"

Me: "What do you mean, you can't disconnect it? Is the FireWire cable stuck?"

She: "I don't think so."

Me: "You don't think so? Have you tried?"

She: "No. I'm afraid to!"

Me: "Why?"

continues on next page

Kelly's Sidebar: "Do not disconnect" *continued*

She: "Because my iPod is flashing this warning sign and says, 'Do not disconnect.' I'm afraid I'll break something if I pull the cable out!"

Me: "Ohhh...."

And that, dear reader, is why this is Kelly's sidebar.

The shortish explanation of why you see this message (or its more-positive partner, the "OK to disconnect" message) is because versions of the iPod that bore software before version 1.2 didn't make it particularly clear when it was and wasn't a good idea to break the FireWire connection between the iPod and computer. More often than not, you'd pull the FireWire cable from the iPod's FireWire port, only to be greeted by a message on your computer screen indicating that you'd severed a vital FireWire connection and you'd be well advised to shove the cable back in at your earliest convenience. (There might have been an "And I mean right *now*, buster!" in there somewhere, too.)

To address this issue, Apple created a warning that makes it abundantly clear that you should not feel at liberty to unplug your iPod whenever the mood strikes. Instead, you should take care to unmount your iPod before unplugging it.

On the Mac, you can do this by selecting the iPod's icon in iTunes and then clicking the Eject iPod button in the bottom-right corner of the iTunes window. Or, on the Mac's Desktop, you can drag the iPod's icon to the Trash.

In Windows, you can click the iPod icon in the Notification area (formerly known as the System Tray) and choose Unmount from the resulting contextual menu. Or you can click the iPod in MusicMatch Jukebox's Device window, select the iPod in the Source list, and click the Eject button in the bottom-left corner of the Device window (or right-click the iPod in the Device window and choose Eject Device from the contextual menu).

After you've unmounted the iPod, the "Do not disconnect" message will change to "OK to disconnect, "signaling that you're welcome to unplug the FireWire cable whenever you like.

But the unspoken question remains: Will your iPod explode (or quietly whimper and die) if you unplug the FireWire cable when the "Do not disconnect" message is displayed?

Probably not. You shouldn't break the connection when the computer is transferring data to the iPod. Doing so could corrupt the hard drive, requiring you to restore the device. If the iPod is just sitting around, merrily charging its battery, it's not likely to suffer terribly if you unplug it. But why take the chance? After all the pleasure your iPod has given you, treat it with respect, and honor its one simple request.

The ultra-really confused iPod

If your iPod won't start up no matter what you've tried, you might be able to make it work again by disassembling the unit (see "It's what's inside that counts: disassembling the iPod" later in this chapter), unplugging the battery and hard drive, plugging the battery and hard drive in again, and reassembling the iPod.

If your iPod is still under warranty, take advantage of that warranty and have your iPod looked at rather than pulling it apart. If Apple learns that you've opened an iPod, there's a possibility that Apple won't honor your warranty.

Secret Button Combinations

By pressing the proper combination of buttons on the iPod's face, you can force the device to reset, enter FireWire disk mode, scan the iPod's hard disk for damage, and perform a series of diagnostic tests. Here are those combinations and the wonders they perform:

- **Reset.** Plug the iPod into a powered FireWire device (the Apple iPod Power Adapter, an auto adapter, or a built-in FireWire port), and press and hold Play and Menu for 10 seconds. When you reset your iPod, your data remains intact, but the iPod restores the factory settings.

  This technique reboots the iPod and is helpful when your iPod is locked up.

- **FireWire disk mode.** Reset the iPod. At the Apple logo, press and hold the Previous and Next buttons.

  Use this technique when you need to mount your iPod on a Mac with an unpowered FireWire card (a FireWire PC Card in your older PowerBook, for example).

- **Disk scan.** Reset the iPod. At the Apple logo, press and hold Previous, Next, Select, and Menu. An animated icon of a disk and magnifying glass with a progress bar below it appears.

  Use this combination when you want to check the integrity of the iPod's hard drive. This test can take 15 to 20 minutes, so be patient. If the scan shows no problems, a checkmark appears over the disk icon. To return your iPod to regular use, press Play.

- **Diagnostic mode.** Reset the iPod. At the Apple logo, press and hold Previous, Next, and Select.

Diagnostic mode includes 16 tests that may help you determine what's wrong with your iPod. See the "Doing Diagnostics" sidebar later in this chapter for more details.

The broken iPod

It's a machine, and regrettably, machines break. If none of these solutions brings your iPod back from the dead, it may need to be repaired. Contact Apple at *http://depot.info.apple.com/ipod/index.html* for instructions on how to have your iPod serviced.

The frozen iPod

Just like a computer, the iPod can freeze from time to time. To thaw it, attach your iPod to a power source—either the power adapter or a powered FireWire port—and press and hold the Play and Menu buttons for 10 seconds.

Failure to charge

There are several reasons why an iPod might not charge. They include:

A Sleeping Computer. The iPod won't charge when it's attached to a sleeping computer. Wake up your computer if you want the iPod to charge.

More than one FireWire device on the chain. Although you can chain multiple FireWire devices together, doing so with an iPod isn't such a hot idea. To begin with, a FireWire device on the chain before the iPod (a hard drive, for example) may be hogging all the power. Second, there have been reports of iPods that have been corrupted when left on a chain with other FireWire devices. To be safe rather than sorry, don't put the iPod on a chain. If you must use multiple FireWire devices, purchase a powered FireWire hub (which costs around $80).

A frozen iPod. An iPod that's frozen won't charge. While the iPod is attached to a power supply, press and hold the Play and Menu buttons.

A faulty FireWire cable. Cables break. Try a different FireWire cable, just in case yours has gone the way of the dodo.

A faulty computer FireWire port. It's possible that the FireWire port on your computer has given up the ghost. Try charging the iPod from the Apple iPod Power Adapter.

A funky power adapter. The Apple iPod Power Adapter could also be bad. Attempt to charge your iPod from your computer.

A faulty FireWire port on the iPod. This is not good. As you plug and unplug the FireWire cable from the iPod's FireWire port, it's possible to put too much stress on the internal connectors that deliver power to your iPod's FireWire port, breaking the bond between those connectors and your iPod's motherboard.

If your iPod is out of warranty, and you're handy with a soldering iron, you could open your iPod (see "It's what's inside that counts: disassembling the iPod" later in this chapter), check for broken connections, and resolder those connections. This kind of repair is one that only the truly skilled should attempt, however.

Broken iPod. I've mentioned this before: iPods occasionally break. If none of these solutions brings your iPod back from the dead, it may need to be repaired. Contact Apple at *http://depot.info.apple.com/ipod/index.html.*

Disk-scan icons at startup

There may come a time when you start up your iPod, and a disc-scan icon appears. This situation occurs when the iPod senses a problem with the hard drive. When the disk scan is complete (a 15 to 20-minute process), you'll see one of four icons. These icons indicate the following conditions:

 • The disk scan failed and will be repeated when you next restart or reset your iPod.

 • Everything's cool. Your iPod's hard drive passed with flying colors.

 • The scan found some problems but was able to fix them. If you see this icon, you should restore your iPod.

 • This is bad. The Sad iPod icon indicates that the iPod can't retrieve data from the hard drive. If you see this icon, it's time to send your iPod to the shop.

 There's actually one more disk-scan icon. This icon indicates that you canceled the disk scan by holding down the Select button for 3 seconds. The next time you switch on your iPod, the disk scan will be repeated.

Doing Diagnostics

Ever wonder what Apple technicians do when they want to test an iPod? Just as you can, they reset the iPod, and when they see the Apple logo, they press Previous, Next, and Select.

When you do this, you'll hear a chirp, very briefly see a splash screen that displays the version of the diagnostic test, and finally see a list of tests. That list includes:

5 IN 1. This test causes the iPod to run tests J through N.

RESET. This test resets the iPod.

KEY. When you activate this test, you have 5 seconds to press all the buttons on the iPod. As you do so, the name of each button appears on the display. Press all the buttons in that 5-second time limit, and the words KEY PASS appear.

AUDIO. This test checks the iPod's audio subsystem. If everything's okay, you'll see 0X00000001 DONE in the display.

REMOTE. This screen is for testing the remote control. As you press each button on the Apple remote control plugged into your iPod, a white bar appears. When all buttons have been pushed successfully, you see the message RMT PASS. If no remote control is plugged into the iPod, you'll see a single white bar across the top of the display, and the only way to regain control of your iPod is to reset the device by pressing Menu and Play for 10 seconds.

FIREWIRE. This test checks the iPod's FireWire port. If everything's okay, you'll see FW PASS in the display.

SLEEP. This test puts the iPod to sleep. When you attempt to wake it, you'll see a low-battery icon. To regain control of your iPod, you must reset it.

A2D. This test checks the iPod's power system. When my 5 GB iPod passed this test, the display read A2D 4.1V 0X000000F8 CHG OK FW 1 BAT 1.

OTPO CNT. When you turn the scroll wheel, its value is displayed in hexadecimal code.

LCM. This display test scrolls through a different pattern when you press Select (three patterns total).

RTC. This test displays a different hexadecimal code each time you press Select. iPoding.com (**www.ipoding.com**) suggests that the test measures the iPod's real-time clock.

SDRAM. This test checks the iPod's onboard RAM. If the iPod passes, you'll see SDRAM PASS in the display.

FLASH. iPoding.com believes that the hexadecimal number that results from this test represents the iPod's ROM version.

WHEELA2D. This test seems to check for scroll-wheel movement. In versions of the iPod software before 1.2, this test is labeled OTPO.

continues on next page

> **Doing Diagnostics** *continued*
>
> **HDD SCAN.** This test initiates the disk-scan test (which can take 15 to 20 minutes).
>
> **RUN IN.** This test runs a series of internal diagnostic tests until you press and hold the Play button to return to the diagnostic screen.
>
> To advance from one test to the next, press the Next button. To move back through the tests, press the Previous button. To activate a test, press the Select button. To return to the diagnostic screen at the end of a test, press the Play button.
>
> To exit diagnostic mode, you must reset your iPod by pressing and holding the Play and Menu buttons for approximately 10 seconds.

Opening the iPod

Come on, admit it—you've always wondered what the inside of your iPod looks like. Please allow me to save you the trouble of finding out on your own. The following pictures and descriptions illustrate how the original iPod is put together and what makes it tick.

Beneath the cover

If you were to perform surgery on your iPod, here's what you'd find.

The battery

The first thing you see when you remove the iPod's back plate is the Sony Fukushima 4.15 lithium polymer battery. This battery, which is about 0.11 inch thick, plugs into the iPod's main circuit board. It's attached to the hard drive with sticky rubber pads.

The hard drive

Depending on the iPod model you've purchased, the Toshiba hard drive underneath the battery holds 5, 10, or 20 GB of data. The drive's detachable data connector is at the bottom of the iPod.

The circuit board

The iPod's circuit board hosts the components necessary for the iPod to do its job. Here, you'll find the following items (**Figure 8.7**):

FireWire controller chip   CPU   SDRAM chip

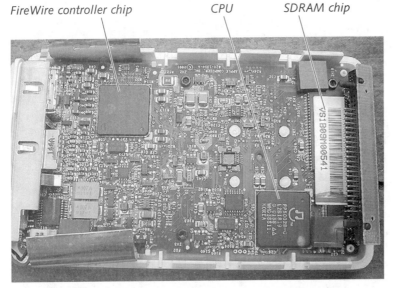

Figure 8.7 The innards of the original iPod and resident chips.

- **The FireWire controller chip.** As the name implies, this Texas Instruments TSB43AA82 chip controls the iPod's FireWire functions.

- **The SDRAM chip.** This 32 MB Samsung K4S561632C chip serves as the iPod's 20-minute music buffer. Music is read from the hard drive and moved into this chip, allowing the hard drive to spin down (thus saving battery power). When the buffer is nearly empty, the hard drive spins back up and loads additional music into the chip.

- **The Central Processing Unit (CPU).** The PortalPlayer PP5002B chip takes care of processing music on the iPod, including encoding and decoding MP3 files and producing effects such as EQ and bass boost.

Can You Upgrade the Hard Drive?

I've made it a habit to disassemble an original iPod whenever I'm called upon to speak about this little digital wonder. Because the folks I address have a strong desire to know what the iPod looks like under the hood (and are more than willing to see someone else risk his iPod to satisfy their curiosity), I do my best to oblige.

Invariably, once the iPod is apart, someone shouts out: "Can I put a higher-capacity hard drive into my iPod?"

Yes, you can. I have successfully transplanted the hard drive from an original 10 GB iPod into the body of an original 5 GB iPod. After the operation, I checked this Frankenpod's About screen, and sure enough, it thought it was a 10 GB iPod. As you would expect, all the data—music, playlists, calendars, and contacts—worked perfectly.

You won't have this kind of luck moving the drive from a 20 GB iPod to a 5 or 10 GB model, however, because the hard drive in the 20 GB iPod is physically larger; it won't fit in the case of a 5 or 10 GB iPod.

Now, before you uncork the champagne and strew confetti from one end of the house to the other, you should understand that, as I write this chapter, the small hard drive inside the iPod costs about as much as the iPod itself. In other words, there's currently no real advantage to upgrading the hard drive. As hard-drive prices diminish (and the iPod's price remains at its current level), upgrading the hard drive might make sense.

It's what's inside that counts: disassembling the original iPod

Note: These instructions are for the original iPod models only. Do not attempt to disassemble one of the iPod models released after July 2002 (see the sidebar "It's What's Inside (That You're Likely to Break) That Counts: Not Disassembling the New iPod" later in this chapter).

My greatest desire is that you'll never feel compelled to open your iPod. But there are occasions when pulling it apart makes sense—when your iPod apparently has given up the ghost, its warranty has expired, or other troubleshooting techniques have failed, and before pungling up more than $255 plus tax for Apple to repair or replace it, you'd like to try one more thing. Here's how to accomplish that one more thing:

1. Turn off the iPod, and engage its Hold switch so that it doesn't turn on while you're working on it.

2. Find a thin piece of smooth plastic a little thinner than a credit card (my library card did the trick).

   You'll use this plastic as a wedge to remove the back plate. Don't use a screwdriver, as it can bend and score the case.

3. Hold the iPod upright, facing you; insert an edge of the plastic between the FireWire port and the symbol for that port; and push forward toward the corner of the iPod.

   If you're left-handed, you'll probably want to start below the Hold switch and push toward the corner nearest to it.

   The corner of the back plate should pull slightly away from the front.

4. With the plastic wedged between the back case and the front, continue pushing around the corner and down the side of the iPod, working the back case away from the front.

   Work slowly; the 12 plastic clips holding the back plate in place can break if you wrench the back plate away too violently.

5. Work the plastic all the way around the back plate, and when the back plate is free, pull it off (**Figure 8.8**).

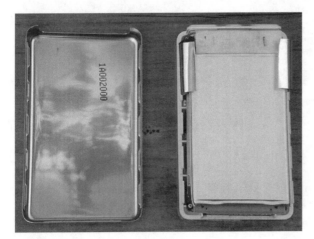

Figure 8.8 The backless iPod.

6. Pull out the battery.

The battery is held in place by a couple of thin sticky rubber pads that are *really* sticky. To dislodge the battery from the hard drive, you must use a fair amount of force. Before applying the force, hold the hard drive in place. If you don't, the hard drive is likely to pull up with the battery, and you could damage the hard drive's data connector (**Figure 8.9**).

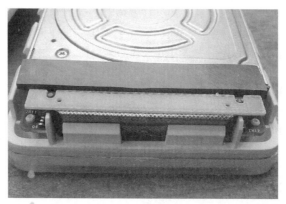

Figure 8.9
The hard-drive connector.

7. Fold the battery away from the iPod so that you can access the hard drive without pulling on the thin battery cables (**Figure 8.10**).

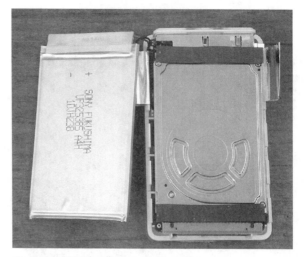

Figure 8.10 The battery laid aside.

8. Gently pull the hard drive away from the iPod's circuit board, pulling from the top first (**Figure 8.11**).

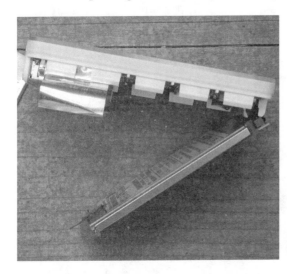

Figure 8.11
Pull the hard drive away from the top of the iPod.

9. When the top and bottom pads are free, detach the hard drive's data connector by grasping it and gently pulling the drive away from the connector (**Figure 8.12**).

Figure 8.12
The hard drive removed.

10. To detach the battery from the circuit board, grasp the top of the white plastic connector with a pair of needle-nosed pliers, and gently pull straight up (**Figure 8.13**).

Figure 8.13
The battery connector.

11. To reassemble the iPod, reattach the battery connector, replace the hard drive and data connector, place the battery back on top of the hard drive, and press the back plate into place.

Be sure that the battery wires are out of the way so the back plate doesn't pinch (or break) them.

It's What's Inside (That You're Likely to Break) That Counts: Not Disassembling the New iPod

After the long look at pulling apart the original 5 and 10 GB iPods, I understand that you might be disappointed to find no instructions for disassembling the latest iPods. Believe me, it's for your (and your iPod's) own good.

Apple changed the case design on the newest iPods so that the metal cover surrounds the FireWire port, Sound Output port, and Hold switch. If you were to follow the instructions I provide for disassembling the original iPod, you'd likely damage the FireWire and audio connections, rendering your iPod permanently kaput. Preferring not to provide the means for your iPod's almost-assured destruction, I will simply suggest that these iPods be disassembled only by those who are trained to do so.

Besides, were you to open one successfully, you'd find only that the motherboard is slightly different and that Apple used a different shock-absorbing scheme.

How Much Abuse Can the iPod Take?

A personal story:

In my duties as a contributing editor for *Macworld* magazine, I was tasked with the job of stress-testing one of the original 5 GB iPods. Because these early iPods didn't ship with a belt clip, case, or armband, my editor felt that it was *Macworld*'s duty to see how much abuse an iPod could take before it finally played its last MP3. Heartbreaking as it was to subject such a beautiful gadget to such treatment, I accepted the assignment.

I devised four tests, each of which involved dropping the iPod onto a hard surface. To replicate real-world situations, I determined to drop the iPod onto a slab of cement from waist-high, drop the iPod while jogging on a paved road, drop the iPod from a bicycle traveling approximately 25 mph, and drop that iPod from that same bicycle at 30 mph. The iPod was playing during all these tests.

Because I didn't have four iPods to sacrifice, I performed the tests on a single iPod—which, of course, calls the results into question due to the factor of accumulated damage. For this reason, I didn't send the results to the Pulitzer committee.

The results were:

- **Dropped from waist-high, with bottom plate facing down.** The iPod continued to play. But the front plastic was dinged, and the back was scratched.

- **Dropped while jogging, with the iPod held with ports facing skyward.** The iPod continued to play. The side of the back case was dented and pulled slightly away from the front. The back plate did not fit snugly after being pushed back into place.

- **Dropped from a bicycle at 25 mph, with the bottom plate facing down.** The iPod continued to play. The back plate was severely scratched and dented. The back plate pulled even farther away from the front. The back plate did not fit snugly after being pushed back into place.

- **Dropped from a bicycle at 30 mph, with the ports facing skyward.** The iPod stopped playing and flew apart in spectacular fashion. The back plate fell off, as did the front scroll wheel and Select button. When reassembled, the iPod displayed the Sad iPod icon and could not be revived.

Depending on whether yours is a glass-half-empty or glass-half-full personality, you can view these results in two ways: You can be disappointed that the iPod eventually died, or you can be impressed that it suffered four separate instances of violent abuse before it finally met its maker.

Personally, I was pleased that the iPod took such a licking and kept on ticking. That doesn't mean, however, that I'd transport my iPod without a padded case equipped with a belt clip.

Thank You

As thanks for purchasing this book, I'd like to give you a little something to put on your iPod. That little something is *Of Eve,* a solo piano album I recorded some years ago.

The music on *Of Eve* belongs to me, but you're welcome to download and place it on your computer and iPod for your personal listening pleasure. You do not, however, have my permission to use this music in a public broadcast or for any commercial purposes without my permission.

You can find your copy here: *www.peachpit.com/ipodsecrets.*

I hope you enjoy it.

Index

B

Backlight Timer setting, 26
backlighting, 12, 26
backups, 107–108
battery
    backlighting and, 26
    described, 214
    detaching from circuit board, 220
    drained, 206
    failure to charge, 211–212
    laptop computers and, 193
    life of, 5
    play time, 5
    removing, 218
    unplugging, 210
Billboard.com site, 35
bit rates, 34
boot disks
    applications stored on, 107
    data storage on, 106–108
    failure to boot, 202, 206–207
    installing Mac OS 9, 97–100
    installing Mac OS X (10.1.x), 97,
        100–102
    installing Mac OS X (10.2.x), 97,
        103–105
    Mac iPod and, 95–97, 105–106
    troubleshooting utilities stored on, 106
    uses for, 105–108
    Windows iPod and, 95–96
Browse window, 18–20
browsers, 118
buffer, RAM, 5, 10, 207
button combinations, 210

C

cables. *See also* connections
    adapter, 186
    cost of, 187
    faulty, 211
    finding, 187
    FireWire, 4–5, 10, 14, 96, 211
    headphone splitter, 188
    HotWire, 194

calendar functions, Mac
    accessing calendar, 21
    alarms. *See* alarms
    automatic calendar transfers, 176–177
    creating calendars, 160–168
    events. *See* events
    exporting calendars to iCal, 168
    iCal application. *See* iCal calendar
        application
    iSync utility, 176–177
    Microsoft Entourage, 164–165, 168
    Palm Desktop, 165–168
    removing calendars from iPod,
        175–176
    scrolling through calendar, 175
    transferring calendars to iPod, 173–175
    vCal files, 158–160
calendar functions, Windows
    accessing calendar, 21
    alarms. *See* alarms
    automatic calendar transfers, 177
    creating calendars, 161, 169–172
    EphPod, 92
    events. *See* events
    Microsoft Outlook, 169–170
    Palm Desktop, 170–172
    removing calendars from iPod,
        175–176
    scrolling through calendar, 175
    transferring calendars to iPod, 173–175
    vCal files, 158–160
calendar management, 157–177. *See also*
        contact management
    accessing calendar, 21
    alarms. *See* alarms
    events. *See* events
    iCalendar standard, 157–158
    multiple calendars, 174
    removing calendars from iPod,
        175–176
    scrolling through calendar, 175
    transferring calendars to iPod, 173–175
    vCal files, 158–160
    vCalendar standard, 157–158
Calendar screen, 21
car stereo systems, 188–191
Carbon Copy Cloner, 103–105